The Healthy Seniors Cookbook

Size - Serve 1 or 2

Ideal Meals and Menus
for People Over Sixty
(Or Any Age)

Large
Print

The Healthy
Seniors
COOKBOOK

Ideal Meals and Menus for People Over Sixty (Or Any Age)

Marilyn McFarlane
With a Foreword By Carol Baird, M.D.

For Alyce Cook —
Warm regards,
Marilyn McFarlane

Hatala Geroproducts • Greentop, Missouri

The Healthy Seniors Cookbook:
Ideal Meals and Menus for People Over Sixty (Or Any Age)
by Marilyn McFarlane

ISBN-13: 978-1-933167-30-5

LCCN: 2007930655

Author's note: Every reasonable effort has been made to ascertain that the recipes in this book are original and unique. Should there be any question concerning this, please notify the publisher so that proper credit can be given in any subsequent edition.

Publisher's note: The recipes and menus contained herein should in no way be a substitute for the advice and counsel of a physician. Any person with special dietary or health needs should consult a physician before changing their dietary regimen.

Cover Design: Shaun Hoffeditz
Cover Photo: Marilyn McFarlane
          - Best-Yet Walnut Bread (page 135)
Composition: Age Positive Editorial Services

To the memory of my mother

Ida Mary McFarlane

Acknowledgments

Without the help of numerous people who are interested in the nutritional needs of senior citizens, this book could not have been written.

My thanks go to those who contributed suggestions from their own files and memories, especially those residents of Rose Villa Retirement Home who shared their stories and recipes.

I am very appreciative of Dr. Carol Baird for her comments and grateful to Carolyn Ostergren, R.D., Kay Girsberger, R.D., and Nancy Thorn, R.D., experienced dietitians who offered their professional advice and opinions on nutrition and tips for good health.

A special remembrance goes to my aunt, Esther MacLaren, now deceased, for her help in contributing and collecting recipes.

Thanks to Ian Kitts and Ellen Rall for their enthusiasm in helping with the recipes to enjoy with grandchildren; and thanks to my husband, John Parkhurst, for his unflagging good humor and willingness to participate in many weeks of recipe testing.

Table of Contents

Foreword

And in the end, it is not the years in your life that count, it is the life in your years.

— Abraham Lincoln

Spoken more than one hundred years ago, the truth of Lincoln's comment is apparent in many patients I have seen in my career as a geriatrician. People are living longer and healthier lives than ever before. The average American life expectancy at birth rose from 47.3 years in 1900 to 76.9 years in 2000.

There are some factors that contribute to health and life expectancy for which we have no control, such as our genetic makeup and gender. We do, however, have control over making sure our nutritional needs are met. Diet and nutrition are important components to adding life to our years, and it is my hope that this book helps you take charge of this portion of your life.

In my practice I have the privilege of making home visits. It is in this setting that I can perform a refrigerator "biopsy." All too often I have come across refrigerators with little or no fresh fruits and vegetables, and cupboards may be stacked with ramen noodles and canned goods. From this I know that I should be worried about whether or not the person is eating properly and getting the right vitamins and minerals. I then provide counsel on overcoming the many barriers to maintaining a healthy, life-enhancing diet. Those barriers include diminished taste, decreased chewing ability, lack of transportation, limited finances, and medications. Also, some people find it more difficult to cook and prepare meals as they may have done in the past. There may be foods they can no longer eat, and they get discouraged.

The Healthy Seniors' Cookbook helps to surmount these barriers. It provides updated recipes and menus reviewed by registered dietitians. Emphasis has been put on the use of spices for flavor rather than the traditional salt and fat. Recipes are included for those who have difficulty chewing. In addition, the recipes are in amounts suitable for smaller appetites and for one or two people.

Wellness is an active process of learning and making choices toward years of quality living. I hope you will use and enjoy this compilation of recipes, dietary information and suggestions garnered from elders who are successfully aging and putting more life in their years.

Carol M. Baird, M.D.
President, Oregon Geriatrics Society
President, Oregon Medical Directors Association

Introduction/How To Use This Book

It was just noon on a blustery Saturday in March when I stopped by my widowed mother's apartment to say hello. She was eating lunch — half a slice of white bread, a small piece of cheese, and a cup of tea.

"That's not much lunch," I said as I removed my coat.

"I know," she answered with a guilty smile. Then she sighed. "But I can't think of anything else to fix and don't have the energy anyway. Neither do most of my friends."

It was then, as I put on an apron and began preparing a hot, tasty vegetable soup, that I decided to write this book.

Eating good food is one of life's great pleasures. That enjoyment shouldn't stop at a certain age; it should continue on into our golden years. Our bodies may require less food to maintain life and energy, but we still need nutrients, fiber and flavorsome meals. The food we eat, and the way we eat it, contribute greatly to the quality of our lives. Eating well is important.

Many older people lose interest in food. They may have trouble chewing or have physical problems that make it difficult to meet their dietary needs. They may be low on energy, or they may be bored. With no one but herself to cook for, the woman living alone often neglects her own meals. The man alone may not know how to prepare a proper meal.

The Healthy Seniors Cookbook was created to change all that. It's packed with recipes, menu ideas and helpful hints. In an easy-to-read, easy-to-use format, it provides six weeks' worth of flavorful menus and simple, fast cooking methods, using a standard oven and range.

We haven't neglected nutrition in preparing this cookbook. All the menus and recipes have been carefully reviewed by a physician who specializes in geriatrics. Many of the recipes were developed by seniors who are looking for shortcuts in meal preparation but do not wish to sacrifice taste and enjoyment. Several recipes are more complex, to add variety, and there are a few intended to be occasional treats.

The pages of this book also contain useful extras, such as hints for shopping, cooking and fitness. You'll find suggestions for those on tight budgets, for people on low-sodium or low-cholesterol diets, and for people who live alone and usually eat alone. All these problems are surmountable. They require some creativity and effort, but the results are worth it. Nothing means more to a high quality of life than the food we consume.

How To Use This Book

The Healthy Seniors Cookbook is divided into two sections: Recipes and Suggested Menus. They're followed by Appendices that list the recipes lowest in cholesterol and sodium, and a list of dishes that grandparents have said they enjoy making for their visiting grandchildren or, even better, sharing the preparation with them.

Most dishes in the Recipes section are included in the Suggested Menus section. You may choose to try a recipe that seems appealing, or you may wish to follow the recommended menu that uses that dish.

In the Menus section, you will find both light and hearty menus for breakfasts and dinners for a six week period. The foods were selected for their combinations of flavor, texture and nutrition, though you may prefer to substitute your own favorites in some cases.

Almost all the dishes are intended to serve one or two people. However, the recipes are easy to increase or decrease, according to the number of servings you need, by doubling or halving the ingredients. All ingredients are generally available throughout the United States and easy to obtain, depending upon the region and season.

These recipes call for little, if any, salt or sugar but plenty of herbs, spices and fiber. This means there is no loss of flavor — in fact, you will find that using herbs and experimenting with them improves the flavor and variety of your diet.

Because seasonings are so important to these recipes, we are providing suggestions for easy ways to use them. Many recipes call for one of our special seasoning combinations: Mixed Herbs, Mixed Hot Spices, or Mixed Sweet Spices. Fix up a batch of each, store them in tightly closed, labeled containers, and you'll be ready for a quick and tasty recipe.

Mixed Herbs
(Makes about 1/3 cup)

3 tablespoons dried sweet basil
1 tablespoon dried marjoram
1 teaspoon dried thyme
1 teaspoon dried oregano

Mixed Hot Spices
(Makes about 1/3 cup)

3 tablespoons chili powder
1-1/2 teaspoons ground cumin
3/4 teaspoon ground cayenne pepper
1/4 teaspoon turmeric

Mixed Sweet Spices
(Makes about 1/3 cup)

3 tablespoons ground cinnamon
1-1/2 teaspoons ground allspice
1-1/2 teaspoons ground cloves
3/4 teaspoon ground ginger
3/4 teaspoon ground nutmeg

Beef

One-Pot Pot Roast
Meat and Potatoes
"No-Peek" Stew
Swiss Steak Special
"Yoganoff" with Zucchini
Raisin Beef
Beef 'N Beans
Meat Loaf
Oriental Beef
Snappy Ginger Beef
Chili Hash
Deep-Dish Spaghetti Bake
Spaghetti With Tomato Sauce
Prime Time Pizza
Goulash
E-Z Ground Beef Casserole
Stuffed Green Peppers
Hamburger Stew

One-Pot Pot Roast
(Serves 2, with leftovers)

Hearty beef and vegetable goodness prepared in a single pot. You can add more vegetables, too --fresh or frozen peas, green beans, or other favorites. Save the leftovers for tomorrow's meal.

> 1 pound boneless beef chuck roast
> 2 teaspoons beef bouillon granules or 2 bouillon
>   cubes, mixed with 3/4 cup water
> 2 tablespoons lemon juice
> 1/2 cup wine, red or white, or 1/2 cup water
> 1 small onion, peeled and sliced
> 1 carrot, sliced
> 1 potato, sliced (peel if you prefer)
> 1 clove garlic, pressed or minced
> 1 teaspoon Mixed Herbs pg. 13
> Bay leaf
> 1/4 teaspoon pepper

Preheat oven to 350°. Place beef in baking dish. Pour bouillon, lemon juice and wine or water over meat. Sprinkle with herbs and pepper. Add vegetables and cover. Bake 1 hour, or until tender.

Tempt Your Appetite:
When food and eating seem a bore, there are several ways to perk up your appetite. A couple of suggestions:
— Take a walk. Even a short walk outside will stimulate your circulation and appetite.
— Set a special table. A pretty place mat, a flower or candle, a cloth napkin and "company" china can make a meal seem more appealing, whether you dine alone or with others.

Meat and Potatoes
(Serves 1)

For those who love a stick-to-the-ribs standby.

1/2 cup cooked, diced beef roast
1/2 cup beef gravy (packaged or left over)
1/4 cup cooked mashed potatoes (instant packaged
    potatoes allow trouble-free preparation but
    are higher in sodium)
2 tablespoons milk
1 teaspoon butter or margarine
1/2 cup cooked carrots or peas
1/2 teaspoon Mixed Herbs

Preheat oven to 350°. Mix beef with gravy in baking dish. Mix in all other ingredients. Bake 15 minutes.

"No-Peek" Stew
(Serves 2 generously)

This melt-in-your-mouth comfort food takes long cooking, but it couldn't be easier to prepare. It's from Edith Owenbey's recipe file; she said "the result is like something from a crockpot."

1/2 pound lean stew beef, cut in bite-sized pieces
1 potato, peeled and cut into chunks
1 carrot, peeled and cut into chunks
Other vegetables as desired
1 can condensed tomato soup, undiluted

Mix all ingredients and place in baking dish. Cover and place in cold oven. Turn oven to 250° and leave for 4-1/2 hours. If more liquid is desired, add water.

Swiss Steak Special
(Serves 2 generously)

Vegetables and meat cook together in a tomato-garlic sauce, combining flavors to create a fine meal in a single pot.

> 1/2 pound round steak or flank steak
> 1 tablespoon flour
> 1/4 teaspoon ground pepper
> 1/2 onion, sliced
> 2 garlic cloves, pressed or minced
> 1 1/2 tablespoons vegetable oil
> 1 bay leaf
> 1/2 teaspoon Mixed Herbs
> 1 potato, peeled and chopped
> 1 carrot, chopped
> 3/4 cup tomato juice (or combined tomato sauce and
>   water)
> 1/2 teaspoon vinegar

Rub flour and pepper on steak. Heat 1/2 tablespoon oil in skillet, add onion and garlic and cook, stirring, until lightly browned. Remove from pan and set aside. Heat remaining tablespoon of oil in skillet and brown steak on both sides. Add onion, seasonings, tomato juice and vinegar. Cover and simmer 1 hour, adding more liquid if needed. Arrange potatoes and carrots around meat. Cover and simmer 20-30 minutes, until vegetables are tender.

Buy Double, Save Trouble
When a recipe calls for one-half pound of ground beef, buy a full pound and make hamburger patties with the other half. Separate the patties with waxed paper and freeze for another meal.

"Yoganoff" with Zucchini
(Serves 2)

Enid Byron shares this taste-pleaser with her neighbors and gets rave reviews. The stroganoff-like sauce is based on lower-calorie yogurt. (For authentic stroganoff, Enid uses sour cream instead of yogurt.)

1/2 pound sirloin or filet of beef, cut in strips
1 tablespoon vegetable oil
1 clove garlic, minced
1/2 cup fresh mushrooms, sliced
1 tablespoon butter or margarine
1 tablespoon flour
3/4 cup beef bouillon or broth
2 tablespoons white wine (optional)
1 teaspoon catsup
1/2 cup sliced zucchini
1/4 teaspoon dill
1/4 cup plain low-fat yogurt

Heat oil in skillet. Sauté beef in oil at medium-high heat, browning all sides. Add garlic and mushrooms and sauté until lightly browned. Remove beef, garlic and mushrooms from pan and set aside. Melt butter in pan and add flour and catsup, stirring until smooth. Add bouillon or broth and simmer, stirring until thickened. Add wine, beef and mushrooms, cover and simmer 45-50 minutes, until tender. Add zucchini and cook another 5 minutes. Stir in dill and yogurt and heat. Do not boil.

Raisin Beef
(Serves 2)

1 tablespoon vegetable oil
3/4 pound lean beef, cut in cubes
2 cloves garlic, minced
1 teaspoon Mixed Herbs
1/2 cup liquid from canned tomatoes, or water
1 potato, peeled and sliced
1 carrot, sliced
Pinch of nutmeg
1/4 cup raisins
1/2 cup canned tomatoes, drained (or fresh, chopped)

Heat oil in skillet and sauté beef cubes until browned on all sides. Add garlic, Mixed Herbs and liquid. Cover tightly and simmer 30 minutes. Add more liquid if needed. Add potato and carrot slices, cover and simmer 20 minutes, until meat and vegetables are tender. Stir in tomatoes, raisins and nutmeg. Simmer, uncovered, until sauce thickens.

Beef 'N Beans
(Serves 2)

1/2 pound lean ground beef
1 cup (9-ounce can) baked beans
1/2 cup crushed pineapple with juice
2 tablespoons brown sugar
1/4 cup catsup

Preheat oven to 350°. Sauté ground beef in skillet until browned. Drain extra fat. Add all other ingredients. Pour into baking dish. Bake 40 minutes.

Meat Loaf
(Serves 2, with leftovers)

A rich, beefy loaf with bread crumbs and a touch of spice. If you're cooking for grandchildren, let them help with the delightfully messy job of mixing the ingredients with their hands. NOTE: Be sure to wash hands thoroughly with hot water and soap after handling raw ground beef.

1 egg
1/2 pound lean ground beef
1/4 cup tomato sauce or stewed tomatoes
3 tablespoons bread crumbs
1 teaspoon soy sauce (optional)
2 tablespoons grated carrot
1 teaspoon lemon rind, grated or minced
1 clove garlic, pressed or minced
Dash pepper

Preheat oven to 375°. Beat egg in a bowl. Add all other ingredients and mix with hands. Place mixture in loaf pan. Bake 45 minutes.

Exercise:
Healthful eating is an important part of maintaining physical fitness. Another part is regular exercise. Scientists say that you may reduce the risk of coronary heart disease by exercising enough to burn 2000 calories per week. You'll feel better, too. Walking, bicycling and swimming are ideal and pleasant forms of exercise. If you walk briskly for 30 minutes, you will expend 150 calories. A leisurely swim will burn 200 calories in 30 minutes, and half an hour of golf consumes 125 calories. If you are not accustomed to exercise, start slowly. Ask your doctor which activity or sport is best for you; then get out and enjoy yourself!

Oriental Beef
(Serves 2)

Crisp vegetables, tender beef, and the tang of ginger hint at the flavor of the Orient. Substitute other vegetables according to taste: green beans, broccoli, water chestnuts and asparagus are good choices. (Tip: Fresh ginger keeps well in the freezer.)

    1 tablespoon vegetable oil
    10-12 strips lean beef
    2 tablespoons sliced onions
    1 carrot, cut in diagonal pieces
    1/4 cup green pepper chunks
    1 teaspoon chopped fresh ginger
    1 garlic clove, chopped or pressed
    1 cup beef broth or bouillon
    1 tablespoon cornstarch
    1 tablespoon soy sauce

Heat oil in skillet or wok. Sauté beef strips until brown. Remove beef from pan. Add more oil if needed and sauté vegetables until tender but still crisp. Stir in ginger and garlic. Add broth or bouillon and beef, cover and simmer 5 minutes. Mix cornstarch with soy sauce and add to beef mixture, stirring until thickened. Serve with rice.

Conserve Energy:
On days when you have more energy, cook enough for more than one meal. Save the extras for the next day or freeze to keep them for a day when you don't feel like cooking — or even thinking about it.

Snappy Ginger Beef
(Serves 2)

2 slices bacon
1/2 medium onion, chopped
3/4 cup beef broth or bouillon
1/4 cup crushed ginger snap cookies
2 tablespoons brown sugar
1 tablespoon vinegar
3/4 cup cooked beef, cut in cubes

Sauté bacon in skillet until crisp. Remove bacon and crumble. Pour grease from skillet, leaving a teaspoonful. Place all other ingredients except beef in skillet. Add crumbled bacon and simmer 5 - 8 minutes. Add beef cubes and simmer until heated through.

Chili Hash
(Serves 2)
Not too hot, not too mild — a beef chili dish that has a just-right touch of spice.

2 teaspoons vegetable oil
1/2 onion, chopped
1/2 green bell pepper, chopped
1/2 pound ground beef
1 cup tomato sauce
1/2 cup water
1/4 cup uncooked brown or white rice
1/2 teaspoon chili powder
1/4 teaspoon oregano
Dash cumin
Dash pepper

Preheat oven to 350°. Heat oil in skillet and sauté onion, green pepper and beef until lightly browned. Drain fat. Stir in all other ingredients. Pour into oiled baking dish. Cover and bake one hour, until rice is tender.

Deep-Dish Spaghetti Bake
(Serves 3-4)

4 ounces spaghetti, cooked
1/2 pound lean ground beef
1/2 onion, chopped
1/2 teaspoon salt
1 clove garlic, pressed or minced
1/4 teaspoon oregano
1 teaspoon sweet basil
Dash hot pepper sauce
1 16-ounce can stewed tomatoes
1/3 cup chopped mushrooms, canned or fresh
1/2 cup grated Parmesan or Romano cheese (or other
      favorite cheese)

Preheat oven to 375°. Sauté ground beef in skillet until browned. Add onion and sauté until tender. Drain fat. Stir in remaining ingredients except spaghetti and cheese and bring to a simmer. Stir in cooked spaghetti. Pour mixture into greased casserole and place in oven. Bake 20 minutes. Sprinkle with grated cheese and bake 5 more minutes.

Spaghetti With Tomato Sauce
(Serves 2 generously)

There's a secret to the tantalizing flavor of this marinara sauce. It's an unusual hint of sweetness.

> 1/2 pound lean ground beef
> 1 tablespoon vegetable oil
> 1/2 onion, chopped
> 1/2 green bell pepper, chopped
> 1 8-ounce can stewed tomatoes or 1 can tomato paste with
>   3 cans water
> 2 cloves garlic, minced
> 1 teaspoon Mixed Herbs
> 1 tablespoon grape jelly
> 4 ounces spaghetti

Sauté ground beef and onions in oil in skillet until meat is browned. Drain fat. Add all other ingredients except spaghetti. Cover and simmer 2 hours, stirring occasionally. Add water if more liquid is needed. Cook spaghetti in boiling water in kettle just until tender. Drain. Serve sauce over spaghetti and sprinkle with Parmesan cheese if desired.

Prime Time Pizza
(Serves 1)

Just right for a no-muss, no-fuss supper while you watch a favorite TV program.

> 3 biscuits from refrigerated package (there are usually 8
>   or 10 to a package — bake them all and save the
>   extras for future meals, or use frozen biscuits)
> 1/3 cup lean ground beef or pork sausage

1 teaspoon vegetable oil
3 tablespoons tomato sauce
Grated cheese
2 tablespoons chopped onion
1 tablespoon Mixed Herbs

Preheat oven to 400°. Place biscuits on ungreased baking sheet. With water glass, press biscuits into flat circles. Sauté ground beef and onion until lightly browned. Add herbs. Top each biscuit with a spoonful each of tomato sauce, meat mixture and grated cheese. Bake 10-12 minutes.
EASY OPTION: Use a toasted English muffin as the pizza base. Pop it under the broiler until the cheese bubbles.

Goulash
(Serves 2 generously)
Vera Porter contributes this recipe for a hearty, flavorful one-dish meal.

2 teaspoons vegetable oil
1/2 pound ground beef
1/2 cup cooked macaroni
2 tablespoons chopped green bell pepper
1 tablespoon steak sauce
1 cup (1 small can) cream-style corn
1/2 can condensed tomato soup
Dash salt and pepper
1/2 cup grated cheddar cheese

Preheat oven to 350°. Heat oil in skillet. Brown ground beef in skillet. Drain fat. Add all other ingredients except cheese and stir. Place in baking dish and sprinkle with cheese. Bake 30-40 minutes.

E-Z Ground Beef Casserole
(Serves 2)

Esther MacLaren's one-dish meal is delicious and quick to fix — a good hot dinner after an afternoon with the book club.

    2 teaspoons vegetable oil
    1/2 pound lean ground beef
    1/2 onion, chopped
    1/4 cup rice
    1-1/2 cups water or beef bouillon
    1 potato, peeled and cubed
    1 carrot, sliced
    1/4 teaspoon salt
    Dash pepper
    2 teaspoons soy sauce

Preheat oven to 350°. Heat oil in skillet. Brown beef and onion in oil. Drain fat. Mix all other ingredients, and pour into baking dish. Bake 30 minutes. (Dish may also be cooked in covered skillet on stove top.)

Stuffed Green Peppers
(Serves 2)

    2 green bell peppers
    2 tablespoons chopped onion
    2 teaspoons vegetable oil
    1/2 pound lean ground beef
    1/2 cup dry bread crumbs
    2 tablespoons grated cheddar cheese
    1 teaspoon Mixed Hot Spices
    1/2 cup tomato sauce
    2 tablespoons water
    1/8 teaspoon salt

Preheat oven to 375°. Slice tops off peppers. Discard stems, seeds and membranes. Chop trimmings. Blanch peppers (about 4 minutes in a pot of boiling water). Heat oil in skillet. Sauté onion and pepper trimmings. Add beef and sauté until browned. Remove from heat. Drain fat. Mix crumbs, cheese and seasonings and add to beef mixture. Spoon into peppers. Place peppers in buttered baking dish. Mix tomato sauce and water and pour over and around peppers. Bake 30 minutes.

Hamburger Stew
(Serves 2)

2 teaspoons vegetable oil
1/2 pound lean ground beef
1/2 onion, chopped
1 celery stalk with leaves, chopped
1 potato, cubed (peel if you prefer; it's not necessary)
1 carrot, chopped
1 garlic clove, sliced
1/4 teaspoon salt
Dash pepper
1 bay leaf
1 beef bouillon cube
1 cup water

Heat oil in saucepan. Sauté ground beef in oil until cooked. Drain fat if necessary. Add all other ingredients. Bring to a boil, then cover and simmer for 20 minutes until potatoes are fork-tender, adding water if needed.

Pork & Ham

Cranberry Pork Steaks
Succotash Ham
Pineapple Sweet and Sour Pork
Sausage with Pepper and Mushrooms
Curried Ham with Fruit
Sugar-and-Spice Ham Loaf
Ham-Stuffed Squash
Supper Salad

Cranberry Pork Steaks
(Serves 2)

Combine meaty pork with the tartness of cranberries for the best flavors of both.

    2 lean pork steaks
    Dash pepper
    2 tablespoons jellied or whole cranberry sauce, fresh or
          canned
    2 slices orange peel (or 1 teaspoon grated peel)

Preheat oven to 350°. Place steaks in baking pan and sprinkle with pepper. Top each steak with cranberry sauce and orange peel. Bake uncovered for 30 minutes or until meat is tender.

Succotash Ham
(Serves 2)

    1/2 onion, chopped
    1 tablespoon butter or margarine
    1/2 cup lima beans, frozen or canned
    1/2 cup water or liquid from beans can
    1/2 teaspoon Mixed Herbs
    1 cup corn, fresh or frozen
    1/2 cup diced, cooked lean ham

Melt butter in saucepan. Sauté onions in butter until yellow. Add water, beans and seasonings and simmer 5-8 minutes. Add corn, cover, and simmer 5 minutes. Add ham cubes and heat.

Pineapple Sweet and Sour Pork
(Serves 2)

1/2 pound lean pork, cut into cubes
1 tablespoon vegetable oil
1/2 cup beef bouillon
Dash pepper
2 tablespoons chopped green pepper
2 tablespoons chopped green onion (scallion)
1/2 cup crushed or chunk canned pineapple
1 tablespoon sugar
1/4 cup juice from pineapple
2 tablespoons vinegar
1 tablespoon cornstarch
1 teaspoon soy sauce

Brown pork cubes in oil in skillet. Add pepper and bouillon and simmer 20 minutes. Add vegetables and pineapple. Mix all other ingredients together, stir and add to pork dish. Simmer 10 more minutes, stirring.

Stretching:
Our bodies were made to move. When we don't stretch and move, we become less flexible and more prone to injury. Slow, easy stretching of our major muscle groups relieves tension and promotes agility.
You can stretch almost any time, anywhere. While watching TV, take regular breaks in which you consciously reach and stretch your arms and legs. Gentle rotate your head; slowly raise and lower your shoulders; breathe deeply. You will feel a sense of relaxation and well-being.

Sausage with Pepper and Mushrooms
(Serves 2)

1 tablespoon vegetable oil
1/4 pound sliced pork sausage
2 tablespoons chopped onion
2 tablespoons chopped bell pepper, red or green
2 tablespoons chopped mushrooms
1 garlic clove, minced
1 tablespoon sherry (optional)
1/4 cup water
1 teaspoon Mixed Herbs
Chopped parsley

Sauté sausage pieces in skillet. Add onions and peppers and sauté until golden brown. Add garlic, herbs, sherry and water. Cover and simmer 5 minutes. Sprinkle with parsley.

Curried Ham with Fruit
(Serves 1)
Spicy and fruity, but not too sweet.

1 slice cooked ham
1/4 cup crushed pineapple with juice (or chopped
        peaches)
1 teaspoon lemon juice
1 teaspoon brown sugar
1/2 teaspoon curry powder

Heat oven to 350°. Mix all ingredients except ham. Place ham slice in baking dish or on piece of aluminum foil with sides turned up to form edges. Pour sauce over ham. Bake 15 minutes.

Sugar-and-Spice Ham Loaf
(1 small loaf)

Serve this lightly spiced ham dish hot or cold; leftovers make excellent sandwich fillings, spread with mustard or mayonnaise.

    1/2 cup dry bread crumbs
    1/3 cup milk
    1 egg, lightly beaten
    1 cup cooked ham, ground or chopped fine
    1 teaspoon brown sugar
    Pinch cloves
    1/4 teaspoon dry mustard

Preheat oven to 350°. Mix bread crumbs, milk and egg. Add all other ingredients and stir gently. Place in oiled loaf pan and bake 40 minutes.

Ham-Stuffed Squash
(Serves 2)

    1 acorn squash
    2 tablespoons cooked lean chopped ham
    2 tablespoons crushed pineapple or cranberry sauce
    1 tablespoon brown sugar or 1 tablespoon orange juice

Preheat oven to 350°. Split squash lengthwise and remove seeds. Place cut sides down on greased baking sheet and bake 30 minutes. Mix all other ingredients. Remove squash halves from oven, turn cut sides up and fill each with ham mixture. Bake 30 minutes, until squash is tender.

Supper Salad
(Serves 1)

1/2 cooked potato, cut in cubes
1 stalk celery, chopped
1 green onion (scallion), chopped
1/3 cup cooked, diced ham
2 tablespoons low-fat mayonnaise
1/4 teaspoon dill
1/2 teaspoon prepared mustard
1 teaspoon vinegar
Parsley

Combine potato, celery, onion and ham. Mix mayonnaise with dill, mustard and vinegar. Combine both mixtures and chill. Garnish with parsley.

Poultry

Chicken Curry
Mustard Cream Chicken
Chicken Salad
Chicken Cacciatore
Chicken á la King
Canton Chicken Wings
Chicken Milano
Chicken Marmalada
Tarragon Chicken
Italian Chicken
Turkey Tetrazzini
Baked Chicken
Chicken Parmesan
Ginger-Coconut Chicken
Chicken With Greens and Tomato
Chicken Liver Special
Stir-Fried Chicken
Stuffed Cornish Game Hen
Chicken-Stuffed Tomato
Sweet and Sour Chicken
Chicken Cobbler
Turkey with Broccoli, Mushrooms and Almonds
Turkey Joes
Turkey Patties with Onion and Sage
Fruit Juice Chicken
Jambalaya Chicken

Chicken Curry
(Serves 2)

Some studies indicate that eating foods containing curry spices, especially turmeric, may help to prevent Alzheimer's disease.

1/2 cup cubed cooked chicken
3 tablespoons onion, chopped
2 tablespoons vegetable oil, butter or margarine
1 clove garlic, pressed or minced
3 tablespoons chopped apple
2 tablespoons flour
1 cup chicken broth or bouillon
1 tablespoon curry powder
1/4 teaspoon turmeric
Dash cayenne pepper
3 tablespoons raisins

Heat 1 tablespoon butter or oil in saucepan over medium heat. Sauté onion in heated butter or oil until golden. Add garlic and apple, stir and remove with onion from pan. Set aside. Pour other tablespoon oil into pan, heat, and stir in flour and seasonings. Cook until bubbly. Add broth, stirring until thick. Add chicken, cooked onion mixture and raisins, and heat. Serve with condiments such as coconut, chopped banana, peanuts and chutney.

Spices versus Digestion
When you're trying to lower salt intake but find certain herbs and spices upsetting, it's hard to avoid a bland, flavorless diet. One answer: Experiment. If you can't tolerate one spice, try another or try smaller quantities. Keep experimenting until you find what suits you and your digestion.

Mustard Cream Chicken
(Serves 2)

Dan Welton, retired engineer, likes the tangy touch of mustard in this chicken dish, his kitchen specialty. "It not only tastes great, it's low in fat," he says.

    3 - 4 chicken pieces, skin removed
    2 tablespoons Dijon-style mustard
    1/4 teaspoon pepper
    1/2 cup chicken broth or bouillon
    1/3 cup low-fat yogurt

Spread mustard over chicken pieces and refrigerate 3 or more hours. Preheat oven to 350°. Place chicken pieces in baking dish and sprinkle with pepper. Add chicken broth. Bake 40 minutes, basting occasionally. Remove from oven and stir in yogurt. Return to oven and heat for 5 minutes.

Chicken Salad
(Serves 2)

    1/2 cup cubed cooked chicken
    1 celery stalk, chopped
    1 teaspoon lemon juice
    2 tablespoons mayonnaise
    1/4 teaspoon tarragon
    Dash salt and pepper
    1 hardcooked egg, cut in chunks
    2 tablespoons chopped almonds or other nuts
    Lettuce

Toss together all ingredients except eggs, nuts and lettuce. Fold in eggs and chill. Arrange on lettuce leaves and sprinkle with nuts.

Chicken Cacciatore
(Serves 1-2)

1 tablespoon vegetable oil
2-3 pieces chicken, skin removed
1 clove garlic, pressed or minced
1/2 teaspoon rosemary
2 tablespoons vinegar
1/2 cup red wine
1/4 teaspoon pepper
2 tablespoons tomato paste
3 tablespoons chicken broth or bouillon

Heat oil in skillet. Sauté chicken pieces until lightly browned. Add garlic. Add rosemary, vinegar, pepper and wine. Simmer uncovered, to reduce liquid. Add tomato paste and broth, or tomato sauce, and simmer 30 minutes, turning chicken pieces occasionally.

Chicken á la King
(Serves 2)

1 tablespoon butter or margarine
1/4 cup chopped celery
1 tablespoon chopped green pepper
1 tablespoon flour
1/2 teaspoon Mixed Herbs
1 cup chicken broth or bouillon
1/2 cup cooked cubed chicken
1/4 cup evaporated milk

Sauté celery and green pepper in butter in saucepan. Stir in flour and herbs. Add chicken broth and stir until thickened. Add chicken and milk and heat just to simmering.

Canton Chicken Wings
(Serves 2)

Betty Lakey, who lives in an Oregon retirement community, enjoys having seven grandchildren nearby. This spicy dish is a favorite with all of them. It's easy to multiply for a crowd.

6 chicken wings, split (when you find them ready-split,
    they may be called "drumettes")
2 teaspoons minced garlic
1/4 cup chili sauce
1/4 cup sweet and sour sauce or 1/2 teaspoon sugar with
    2 tablespoons red wine vinegar
1 tablespoon red wine vinegar if using sweet and
    sour sauce
2 teaspoons soy sauce
1 teaspoon Chinese Five-Spice seasoning
Dash of Tabasco or other hot sauce.

Combine all ingredients in bowl. Cover and marinate in refrigerator for 2 hours. Preheat oven to 400°. Place in baking pan (can be lined with foil). Bake uncovered 45 minutes. Serve sprinkled with toasted sesame seeds and chopped green onions.

Drugs and Alcohol

If you're on medication, it's generally wise to avoid drinking alcohol. It can be dangerous to your health to mix tranquilizers, painkillers, antibiotics, antihistamines or other drugs with alcohol. Don't drink while you're taking drugs without your doctor's approval.

Chicken Milano
(Serves 2)

1 cup cooked chicken, cubed
1 tablespoon vegetable oil, butter or margarine
2 tablespoons chopped onion
1 1/2 tablespoons flour
Dash pepper
1 clove garlic, minced or pressed
1/4 teaspoon salt
1 cup chicken broth or bouillon
2 tablespoons peas, fresh or frozen
1 tablespoon sherry wine (optional)
2 tablespoons grated Parmesan cheese
1 cup cooked brown rice

Melt butter in saucepan. Sauté onion and garlic in butter or oil until golden (do not brown). Add salt, pepper and flour and stir until bubbly. Add broth and simmer, stirring, until mixture thickens. Add peas, cover and simmer 5 minutes. Add chicken and sherry and heat. Spoon over rice and sprinkle with cheese.

Chicken Marmalada
(Serves 1)

1/2 chicken breast
1 tablespoon orange marmalade
1 teaspoon orange juice
1 teaspoon Dijon-style mustard

Preheat oven to 375°. Place chicken in small baking dish. Mix all other ingredients and pour over chicken. Bake 30 minutes or until no pink shows in center of chicken.

Tarragon Chicken
(Serves 2)

4 pieces chicken
2 tablespoons butter, margarine or vegetable oil
2 tablespoons flour
1/4 teaspoon salt
1/8 teaspoon pepper
1/8 teaspoon paprika
1/4 teaspoon tarragon

Preheat oven to 400°. Melt butter or oil in baking pan in oven. Mix flour and herbs in bowl. Dip chicken pieces in flour mixture, covering all sides. Place chicken in single layer in baking pan. Bake 30 minutes. Turn chicken pieces and continue baking 10-12 minutes, until tender. For crisp skin, broil 3 to 4 minutes after chicken is cooked.

Italian Chicken
(Serves 1)

1/2 chicken breast (can be skinless)
1/4 cup canned diced tomatoes
1/4 cup red wine
2 tablespoons chopped onion
1 garlic clove, minced

Preheat oven to 375°. Place chicken breast in small baking dish. Mix all other ingredients and pour over chicken. Bake 30 minutes, until chicken shows no pink in the center.

Turkey Tetrazzini
(Serves 2)

4 ounces spaghetti, cooked
1/2 cup cooked diced turkey
1/4 cup fresh mushrooms, chopped
2 tablespoons butter or margarine
1 tablespoon flour
1/2 cup turkey or chicken broth or bouillon
1/4 cup milk
1 tablespoon sherry wine (optional)
1/4 teaspoon sage
Dash pepper
2 tablespoons grated Parmesan cheese

Preheat oven to 325°. Melt butter in saucepan. Sauté mushrooms and remove from butter. Stir flour into butter and heat until mixture bubbles. Add broth and stir over low heat until thickened. Add milk, sherry and seasonings. Stir in turkey, mushrooms and cooked spaghetti. Place mixture in baking dish and top with cheese. Bake uncovered 15 minutes, until golden brown.

Freezer and Microwave: If You Have Them, Use Them
Two conveniences that make life in the kitchen easier are the freezer and microwave oven. If you have either or both of these appliances, take advantage of them. Buy ground beef or chops in volume and freeze serving-size quantities. When you make soup, double the quantity and freeze half of it. Frozen foods thaw swiftly and cooking time is cut with a microwave.

Baked Chicken
(Serves 1)

Versatile chicken is here popped into the oven and left to turn brown and tender. Save the bones for delicious homemade soup.

2 pieces chicken with skin removed
1 teaspoon vegetable oil
1 teaspoon butter or margarine
1/4 teaspoon Mixed Herbs
Dash pepper
1 garlic clove, pressed or minced
2 tablespoons lemon juice
1 tablespoon honey

Preheat oven to 350°. Heat butter and oil in baking pan in oven until butter melts. Sprinkle chicken pieces with herbs and pepper. Dip each chicken piece in melted butter and oil and turn. Bake 30 minutes. Mix garlic, lemon juice and honey in bowl. Pour over chicken and return dish to oven for 10-15 minutes, until chicken is cooked.

Vinegar, The Kitchen Helper

Lowly, inexpensive vinegar can be used in many ways other than cooking. Use it (2 or 3 tablespoons) when hand-washing dishes, along with your regular detergent, to make dishes shine. Rinse jars for food storage with a mixture of water and vinegar to eliminate odor. Clean appliances and counter tops with full-strength vinegar to cut through grease and grime. Wipe the rubber tubing on the refrigerator door, as well as the refrigerator interior, with vinegar; this helps prevent mildew. Freshen your coffee maker by running it through a cycle with vinegar and water — then rinse. Use full-strength vinegar to remove fruit and vegetable stains from fingers and dishes.

Chicken Parmesan
(Serves 1-2)

2 pieces chicken, skin removed
1/2 cup soft bread crumbs
1/4 cup grated Parmesan cheese
1 clove garlic, pressed or minced
1/4 teaspoon salt (1/2 teaspoon garlic salt may be
      substituted and garlic omitted)
Dash pepper
2 tablespoons vegetable oil or melted butter

Preheat oven to 350°. In a bowl, mix all ingredients except chicken and oil or butter. Dip chicken pieces in oil or butter, then in crumb mixture, coating well. Place chicken in single layer in baking pan. Bake 45 minutes or until chicken is cooked through but tender.

Ginger-Coconut Chicken
(Serves 1-2)

2 pieces chicken with skin removed
1 tablespoon vegetable oil
2 tablespoons plain yogurt
1 tablespoon prepared mustard
2 tablespoons chopped or flaked coconut
1/2 teaspoon chopped fresh ginger
Dash salt

Heat oil in skillet. Sauté chicken pieces until golden brown. Pour off excess fat, cover and cook over low heat 20 minutes. Mix yogurt, mustard, ginger and salt and pour over chicken. Continue cooking, uncovered, 5 minutes. Sprinkle with coconut before serving.

Chicken With Greens and Tomato
(Serves 2)

2 tablespoons butter or vegetable oil
3-4 pieces chicken
1 clove garlic, minced or pressed
1 green onion (scallion), chopped
1/2 green bell pepper, chopped
2 tablespoons chopped parsley
1/2 teaspoon Mixed Herbs
1/2 cup fresh or canned tomatoes, chopped

Preheat oven to 350°. Heat butter or oil in skillet. Sauté chicken until browned on all sides. Place chicken in baking dish. Add all other ingredients. Cover and bake 40 minutes. If sauce is too thin, thicken with a spoonful of flour mixed with a little cold water.

Chicken Liver Special
(Serves 2)

1 tablespoon vegetable oil
1/4 pound chicken livers
1/2 onion, chopped
1/4 cup chicken broth or bouillon
1/4 teaspoon fresh chopped ginger
1/4 teaspoon sugar
1/4 teaspoon lemon juice

Heat oil in skillet. Sauté onion in hot oil until soft. Add livers and sauté 5 minutes. Add all other ingredients and simmer 5 minutes. If sauce is too thin, thicken with 1 teaspoon cornstarch dissolved in water.

Stir-Fried Chicken
(Serves 2)

1/2 cup chopped broccoli
1 tablespoon vegetable oil
1 garlic clove, minced
1/2 teaspoon fresh ginger, minced
2 tablespoons bean sprouts, fresh or canned
2 tablespoons water chestnuts, sliced
1/4 cup snow peas
1/2 cup chicken broth or water
1/2 tablespoon soy sauce
1 cup cooked chicken, cut in strips

Heat vegetable oil in skillet or wok. Add broccoli and cook, stirring, until broccoli is bright green — about 3 minutes. Stir in garlic and ginger. Add all other ingredients and cook, stirring, until heated through.

Stuffed Cornish Game Hen
(Serves 2)

1 game hen (thaw if frozen)
1/2 onion cut in small chunks
1/2 celery stalk in chunks
Juice of 1/4 lemon
1/2 teaspoon Mixed Herbs
2 tablespoons melted butter

Preheat oven to 350°. Place hen in small roasting pan. Pour lemon juice into hen. Stuff hen with onion, celery, herbs and squeezed lemon section. Drizzle with melted butter. Roast one hour, basting occasionally with pan juices.

Chicken-Stuffed Tomato
(Serves 1)

This easy dish is fun to prepare with a grandchild who likes fresh tomatoes. (Just double the ingredients.) Children like scooping out the tomato jack o'lantern style (it is likely to be messy, but grandparents don't mind that, do they?). If you are feeling ambitious, you could even carve a face on the tomato, and top it with parsley or celery leaf "hair."

1/3 cup diced, cooked chicken
2 teaspoons mayonnaise
1 teaspoon lemon juice
1 teaspoon chopped parsley
1/2 celery stalk, chopped
1 tablespoon chopped water chestnuts (optional)
1 fresh tomato
Lettuce

Combine all ingredients except tomato and lettuce. Slice top from tomato and scoop out seeds and flesh, leaving a thick shell. Chop tomato flesh and add to chicken mixture. Spoon into tomato shell and serve on lettuce.

Be Sociable

Mealtime is a social time. You'll enjoy eating far more if you have company. Invite a neighbor or friend to join you for dinner. Share a potluck with a neighbor. Cultivate new and old acquaintances and keep your zest for food and friends alive.

Sweet and Sour Chicken
(Serves 2)

Serve this quick and easy dish with rice and a crisp green vegetable.

1 cup cooked chicken, cut in bite-size pieces
2 tablespoons prepared mustard
2 tablespoons honey
2 tablespoons lemon juice
1 teaspoon soy sauce
1 1/2 teaspoons vinegar

Combine all ingredients in bowl and stir to coat chicken pieces. Place in skillet or saucepan and simmer 5-8 minutes

Chicken Cobbler
(Serves 1)

1 tablespoon butter or oil
1 tablespoon flour
3/4 cup chicken broth or bouillon
1/4 teaspoon salt
1/4 teaspoon Mixed Herbs
1/3 cup cooked, diced chicken
2 tablespoons peas, fresh or frozen
2 biscuits, uncooked (packaged refrigerated or homemade)

Preheat oven to 400°. Heat butter or oil in saucepan. Stir in flour, salt and herbs. Stir in broth or bouillon and simmer to thicken. Add chicken and peas. Pour mixture into baking dish or small pie pan. Flatten biscuits slightly and place on chicken mixture. Bake 15 minutes, until biscuits are golden brown.

Turkey with Broccoli, Mushrooms and Almonds
(Serves 2)

Rosemary Webster finds this a flavorsome way to make use of leftover turkey. Serve it with a crunchy green salad, and you'll have a fine meal.

2 tablespoons oil or butter
2 tablespoons flour
3/4 cup chicken or turkey broth or milk
1/4 cup chopped mushrooms, fresh or canned
1/4 cup chopped celery
1/4 cup cut-up fresh or frozen broccoli
1 cup cut-up cooked turkey or 3/4 cup ground
     cooked turkey
1 tablespoon sherry wine (optional)
Dash salt and pepper
2 tablespoons chopped toasted almonds

Preheat oven to 400°. Heat butter or oil in saucepan. Stir in flour. Add broth or milk and stir; mixture will be thick. Stir in all other ingredients except almonds. Place in baking dish and bake 15 minutes. Sprinkle with almonds.

Buy Small
If you don't plan to freeze extras or use leftovers, buy only what you need, to avoid waste and expense. Unless you will use that extra cup of canned corn within a day or two, it's better to buy a smaller sized can. Otherwise it will probably sit in your refrigerator until it's too old to use.

Turkey Joes
(Serves 2)

Here's another dish, a turkey version of the ever-popular sloppy joe, to make with the grandchildren. They'll like digging their hands in to squeeze the ingredients together, scooping the cooked food onto buns and, the best part, eating with gusto.

1/2 pound ground turkey
1 egg, lightly beaten
1/4 cup dry bread or cracker crumbs
1 tablespoon Italian-style salad dressing
Dash pepper
1 tablespoon vegetable oil
1/2 cup tomato sauce
1/4 teaspoon sweet basil

In a bowl, mix all ingredients with hands. Heat oil in skillet. Turn turkey mixture into skillet and cook over medium-high heat, stirring occasionally. Serve on buns, sloppy joe style.

Turkey Patties with Onion and Sage
(Serves 2)

1/2 pound ground turkey
1/2 teaspoon ground sage
1 tablespoon minced onion
Dash salt and pepper
1 tablespoon vegetable oil

Mix all ingredients except oil. Form patties. Heat oil in skillet. Sauté patties in hot oil 8 minutes on each side or until cooked through.

Fruit Juice Chicken
(Serves 2)

As the chicken bakes, the fruit juices bubble around it, creating a sauce that is tangy, with a hint of sweetness — a perfect complement to tender, moist chicken.

        2 chicken breast halves, with skin removed
        1 tablespoon melted butter or margarine
        1/4 teaspoon salt
        1/8 teaspoon pepper
        1/2 teaspoon fresh chopped ginger (optional)
        1/2 cup grapefruit juice
        1/2 cup pineapple juice

Preheat oven to 350°. Place chicken breasts in baking pan. Pour butter over and sprinkle with salt and pepper. Pour juices over chicken. Add ginger. Bake 45 minutes.

Losing Weight
If you are heavier than your ideal weight, consult your doctor or dietitian and plan a weight-loss diet. If you exercise, eat wisely, and cut down on fats and sugar, the extra pounds will melt away. A few tips for losing weight:
— Don't skip meals. Eat three small meals a day and snack on low-calorie foods such as carrots, celery and fruits.
— Eat fish and poultry more frequently than red meat.
— Keep busy; don't eat out of boredom.
— Don't deprive yourself. With your doctor or dietitian work out a diet that includes your favorite foods.
— Avoid alcohol; drink plenty of water and fruit juices.

Jambalaya Chicken
(Serves 2 with leftovers)

1 tablespoon vegetable oil
1 stalk celery, chopped
1/4 cup chopped onion
1/4 cup chopped green pepper
1/2 cup uncooked white rice
1 cup chicken broth or bouillon
1 clove garlic, chopped or pressed
Dash cayenne pepper
1 cup cooked chicken, cut in cubes

Heat oil in skillet. Sauté celery, onion and green pepper in oil until lightly browned. Add all other ingredients except chicken. Cover and simmer 20 minutes, until rice is tender. Stir in chicken and simmer 5 minutes.

58

Seafood

Poached Halibut
Fish Fillet Vinaigrette
Fish With Lemon
Dilly Yogurt Fish
Fish With Herbs and Lemon Sauce
Spicy Red Snapper
Ginger Snapper
Curried Fish Bites
Fish On Spinach
Fish in Creamy Mushroom Sauce
Tasty Tuna
Baked Fish With Mushrooms and Tomato
Salmon With Cheese
Spicy Fish Stew
Tuna-Vegie Dish
Salmon Steaks Superb
Slim Shrimp Louis
Doctor Bob's Salmon Loaf
Fish-Stuffed Peppers
Tuna On A Muffin
Tuna Loaf
Tuna au Gratin
Shrimp-Corn Curry

Poached Halibut
(Serves 2)

1/2 stalk celery, chopped
1/8 teaspoon fennel seed
2 sprigs parsley
1 bay leaf
1 cup dry white wine, water, or fish stock
1/2 medium onion, thinly sliced
2/3 pound halibut steak
1 tablespoon butter or olive oil
1 clove garlic, diced
1/2 cup fish or vegetable stock
1 tablespoon chopped parsley
1/2 teaspoon capers
1 teaspoon vinegar

Place celery, fennel seed, sprigs of parsley, bay leaf, wine and one-half of chopped onion in skillet. Bring to a boil and simmer 10 minutes. Place halibut in hot liquid, cover and simmer over low heat until fish is cooked through (10 minutes per inch of steak — do not overcook). While halibut is poaching, heat butter or oil in another skillet. Sauté the other half of chopped onion and garlic until golden brown. Add fish or vegetable broth, chopped parsley, capers and vinegar. Simmer broth mixture for 5 - 8 minutes, adding a spoonful of poaching liquid if needed. Discard poaching liquid and serve fish with sauce.

Mercury In Fish
Studies show that some fish, especially tuna, swordfish, shark, king mackerel and tilefish, can contain high levels of mercury. To be on the safe side, experts advise eating no more than 6 ounces of tuna per week.

Fish Fillet Vinaigrette
(Serves 2)

A low-sodium, low-cholesterol dish that gives a tangy boost to nutritious seafood.

    2 fish fillets, fresh or frozen and thawed
    1 tablespoon vinegar
    2 tablespoons vegetable oil
    1/4 teaspoon crumbled dry tarragon or 1/2 teaspoon
            fresh tarragon
    1/8 teaspoon black pepper
    Pinch paprika
    2 tablespoons grated Parmesan or Swiss cheese (optional)

Heat oven to 400°. Mix vinegar, oil, tarragon, pepper and paprika to make vinaigrette. Place 1 tablespoon vinaigrette in baking dish. Place fillets in baking dish. Spoon sauce over fillets until coated. Bake 12 minutes, until fish is tender and flakes easily. Sprinkle with grated cheese; return to oven to melt cheese.

Accessorize
Just as a touch of jewelry adds interest to clothing, so "accessories" add interest to food. The possibilities are endless. Try these, for example:
— chopped nuts on cooked broccoli
— cinnamon or nutmeg on yogurt
— dash of hot pepper sauce in tomato juice
— chopped chives over scrambled eggs
— mint leaves in cucumber salad
— chili pepper in split-pea soup
— crushed ginger snap cookies on fruit

Fish With Lemon
(Serves 1)
A simple fish dish for lemon lovers.

1 fillet of firm-fleshed white fish
3 slices of lemon
2 teaspoons melted butter
1 tablespoon white or sherry wine or chicken broth
Salt and pepper

Preheat oven to 375°. Place fish on sheet of aluminum foil. Place lemon slices over fish. Add butter and wine or broth and sprinkle lightly with salt and pepper. Fold edges of foil tightly over fish. Bake 10-12 minutes (10 minutes per inch of fish thickness).

Dilly Yogurt Fish
(Serves 2)

1/2 pound fish fillets (thawed, if frozen)
1/4 cup dry white wine
1/2 chicken bouillon cube with 2 tablespoons water
     or chicken broth
1/4 teaspoon dill
Dash pepper
2 tablespoons plain yogurt

Preheat oven to 350°. Place fillets in baking dish. Pour all ingredients except yogurt over fillets. Bake 20 minutes, basting occasionally. Drain liquid from cooked fish into saucepan and simmer until it reduces to about 1/3 cup. (For additional flavor, add a spoonful of chopped mushrooms and onions.). Stir in yogurt and heat (do not boil). Serve sauce over fish.

Fish With Herbs and Lemon Sauce
(Serves 2)

1/2 pound fish fillets
1 tablespoon butter or margarine
2 tablespoons chopped onion or shallots
Dash salt
1 teaspoon Mixed Herbs
2 teaspoons lemon juice
1 teaspoon cornstarch
1/4 cup white wine or chicken or fish broth
1 egg yolk, beaten
1 tablespoon chopped toasted almonds

Preheat oven to 400°. Sauté fish fillets and onion in butter for 3 minutes, turning fish once. Mix together all other ingredients except nuts in saucepan and cook, stirring, until thickened. Place fish and onions in baking dish and pour sauce over. Bake until sauce bubbles, about 10 minutes. Sprinkle with chopped toasted almonds

Drugs and Food

When you are taking medication, be aware of how drugs interact with foods. What you eat has an effect on the way drugs behave in your body, and some drugs may promote dietary deficiencies. Three popular drugs, antacids, aspirin and laxatives, are examples. The aluminum hydroxide in antacids can contribute to phosphate deficiency. Aspirin can cause bleeding in the gastrointestinal tract. Laxatives can affect the absorption of vitamin D or deplete bone phosphorus. If you take aspirin to ease arthritis pain, for example, you may need a diet higher in iron and should consult your doctor about it.

Spicy Red Snapper
(Serves 2)

1/2 pound red snapper (or other firm white fish, like cod)
2 tablespoons Worcestershire or steak sauce
1 tablespoon catsup
1 tablespoon vegetable oil
1 teaspoon vinegar
1/4 teaspoon curry powder

Cut fish into bite-sized pieces and place in greased baking pan. Combine all other ingredients and pour over fish. Broil 3 inches from heat for 4 minutes. Turn and brush with sauce. Broil 4 minutes longer, until fish is tender.

Ginger Snapper
(Serves 2)

Not the cookie variety, but a well-seasoned, gingery red snapper, its sauce an excellent complement to the nutritious fish.

1/2 pound red snapper fillet
1/4 teaspoon pepper
1 tablespoon vegetable oil
2 tablespoons chopped onion
1 clove garlic, chopped or pressed
1 teaspoon chopped fresh ginger
2 tablespoons sherry or white wine

Cut fish into strips or bite-sized pieces and sprinkle with pepper. Sauté onion in oil in skillet until lightly browned. Remove onion and set aside. Sauté fish in hot oil until golden brown. Stir in ginger and garlic. Add wine and simmer 5 to 8 minutes, until fish flakes easily with fork.

Curried Fish Bites
(Serves 2)

1/2 pound white fish fillet, cut in bite-sized pieces
2 tablespoons flour
1 tablespoon wheat germ
1 teaspoon curry powder
Dash cayenne pepper
1 tablespoon vegetable oil
1 tablespoon butter of margarine
1/4 cup chopped nuts
Parsley

Mix flour with seasonings and wheat germ. Coat fish pieces with flour mixture. Heat oil and butter in skillet. Sauté fish until lightly browned on all sides, about 10 minutes. Sprinkle nuts on fish and garnish with parsley.

Fish On Spinach
(Serves 2)

1 tablespoon vegetable oil
1/2 pound white fish fillets
1 tablespoon lemon juice
1 cup chopped spinach, fresh or frozen and thawed
Dash salt and pepper
1/4 teaspoon nutmeg
2 tablespoons grated Swiss cheese

Preheat oven to 350°. Heat oil in skillet. Sauté fish in oil until lightly browned. Place spinach in buttered baking dish. Place fish on spinach bed. Sprinkle with seasonings and cheese. Bake 10-12 minutes or until fish is cooked and flakes easily.

Fish in Creamy Mushroom Sauce
(Serves 2)

2 1/2 tablespoons butter or vegetable oil
2 tablespoons flour
1 cup milk
Dash salt and pepper
1/2 pound fish fillets (any firm, white fish)
2 tablespoons butter or margarine
1/2 onion, chopped
1/2 cup chopped mushrooms
1/4 teaspoon Pistol River mushroom seasonings (optional)

Melt 1 1/2 tablespoons butter or oil in saucepan. Add flour, salt
and pepper and heat, stirring constantly, until bubbly. Add milk
and heat, stirring, until thickened. Melt 1/2 tablespoon butter
in skillet. Sauté onions and mushrooms in butter until lightly
browned, and stir into white sauce. Cut fish into bite-sized pieces.
Melt 1/2 tablespoon butter in skillet. Sauté fish pieces in butter
until golden brown and cooked through. Add fish to sauce. Serve
over rice.

Chewing Solutions
When chewing is a problem or dentures give you trouble, you can
still enjoy eating. Try a variety of softer foods (mashed potatoes,
eggs, cottage cheese, oatmeal, cream of wheat, applesauce, gelatin,
banana). Use tools for the work your teeth can't do. Grind or
chop fruits, vegetables and meats in a grinder, blender or food
processor. Your kitchen knife can help, too. Use it to chop raw
foods finely instead of serving them whole or sliced.

Tasty Tuna
(Serves 1)

Simple to prepare, yet packed with protein, vitamins and flavor.

1/2 cup canned tuna
1/3 cup cracker crumbs
1 tablespoon chopped onion
2 tablespoons chopped celery
1 tablespoon mayonnaise, sour cream or yogurt
1/8 teaspoon pepper
Slice of cheddar or Swiss cheese

Preheat oven to 325°. Mix all ingredients except cheese in baking dish. Top with cheese. Bake 20 minutes.

Baked Fish With Mushrooms and Tomato
(Serves 2)

1/2 pound white fish fillets
2 tablespoons lemon juice
1 sliced tomato
1/2 cup sliced mushrooms, fresh or canned, drained
1/2 teaspoon Mixed Herbs
1/2 onion, chopped
1 tablespoon vegetable oil or butter

Preheat oven to 350°. Place fish fillets in baking dish and pour lemon juice over. Add tomato slices, mushrooms, herbs and onion. Drizzle with oil or butter. Cover and bake 10 minutes. Uncover and bake 10 more minutes.

Salmon With Cheese
(Serves 2)

A light casserole, fine for lunch or an easy-to-fix dinner.

- 1 tablespoon butter or margarine
- 1 tablespoon flour
- 1/2 cup canned salmon or fresh, cooked salmon
- Liquid from salmon, if canned, and water to equal ½ cup
- 1/8 teaspoon salt
- 1/8 teaspoon pepper
- 1/4 teaspoon dill
- 2 tablespoons bread crumbs, buttered
- 2 tablespoons grated cheese

Preheat oven to 400°. Melt butter in saucepan. Stir in flour, salt, pepper and dill, and heat until bubbly. Add liquid and stir until thick. Add salmon. Place mixture in baking dish or custard cups. Top with bread crumbs and cheese. Bake 12 - 15 minutes, until hot and bubbly.

Fish Oil
Remember the old-fashioned tonic, cod liver oil? Scientists are finding that Grandma was right: Oil from fish supplies substances that can reduce blood pressure, lower cholesterol, and protect against some diseases. To get the benefits of omega-3 fatty acids, many nutritionists recommend eating fish two or three times a week.

Spicy Fish Stew
(Serves 2)

1 cup (one 8-ounce can) stewed tomatoes with liquid
    (Cajun-style is best)
1/4 cup water
1 small potato, chopped
1/2 cup chopped celery
1/2 cup chopped onion
1/2 pound firm-fleshed white fish, cut in bite-sized pieces
1/4 teaspoon Mixed Hot Spices

Place tomatoes, liquid and water in saucepan and bring to boil. Add potatoes, cover and cook until nearly tender (about 8 minutes). Add all other ingredients, cover and simmer 10 minutes.

Tuna-Vegie Dish
(Serves 2, with leftovers)

1 celery stalk, sliced
1/2 tablespoon chopped onion
1/2 cup water
1/2 teaspoon Mixed Herbs
1 cup canned tomatoes
1/2 cup uncooked brown or white rice
1 can tuna, drained

Mix celery, onion, water, herbs and tomato liquid in skillet and bring to boil. Add rice and bring to boil. Cover and simmer 20 minutes for white rice, 30 minutes for brown. Add tomatoes and tuna and heat.

Salmon Steaks Superb
(Serves 2)

2 fresh salmon steaks, preferably wild salmon
1/4 cup sliced fresh mushrooms
1 tablespoon butter of margarine
1/4 cup white wine
Dash salt and pepper
Hollandaise Sauce (page 87)

Melt butter in skillet. Sauté mushrooms in butter until slightly tender, about 4 minutes. Remove mushrooms from pan and set aside. Sauté salmon until light golden brown (add more butter if necessary). Add wine, seasonings and mushrooms and simmer 10 minutes. Serve with warm Hollandaise Sauce.

Slim Shrimp Louis
(Serves 1 generously)

Here's an easy, low-calorie, tasty shrimp salad. Sprinkle in a few capers for additional zip.

1/2 cup cooked bay shrimp, chilled
1 teaspoon low-fat mayonnaise
1 teaspoon non-fat yogurt
1/2 teaspoon catsup
1/2 teaspoon vinegar
1/4 teaspoon horseradish
Salt and pepper

Mix all ingredients except shrimp. Fold in shrimp. Serve on lettuce, with tomato wedges, olives and lemon slices.

Doctor Bob's Salmon Loaf
(Serves 2)

Dr. Robert McFarlane, fully enjoying retirement, likes to cook with the regional bounty of his native Pacific Northwest. This soufflé-like loaf is a favorite.

> 3 tablespoons butter
> 4 tablespoons flour
> 1 cup milk
> Dash salt
> 2 cups cooked, flaked salmon, fresh or canned
> 1 cup bread crumbs
> 1 tablespoon lemon juice
> 2 tablespoons minced parsley
> 2 tablespoons grated onion
> 2 eggs, separated

Preheat oven to 350°. Melt butter in saucepan. Add flour and salt and stir until bubbly. Add milk and stir until thickened. In a bowl, beat egg whites until stiff peaks form. Set aside. Beat egg yolks and stir into white sauce. Stir in bread crumbs and all other ingredients except egg whites. Fold in egg whites. Spoon mixture into buttered loaf pan. Bake 30 - 40 minutes. Serve with hollandaise or tomato sauce.

Balance Your Cholesterol Level

Numerous studies show that simple diet changes can help to lower your cholesterol. A few: Eat less red meat and more fish. Avoid egg yolk, go for the vegetables and fruits. Eat more nuts (except peanuts), soy foods and garlic. Use olive oil instead of butter or other saturated fats. Get plenty of fiber — oats, whole grains, and vegetable fibers.

Fish-Stuffed Peppers
(Serves 2)

2 green or red bell peppers
1/2 cup cooked fish, flaked
1/4 cup chopped onion
1/4 cup bread crumbs
1 tablespoon lemon juice
1/4 teaspoon salt
Dash pepper
1/2 cup tomato sauce
1/2 teaspoon dill

Preheat oven to 350°. Cut tops from peppers and remove seeds and membranes. Blanch peppers for 3 minutes in simmering water in saucepan. Mix fish, onion, crumbs, lemon juice, salt and pepper. Add dill to tomato sauce. Stuff peppers with fish mixture and place in baking dish. Pour sauce over. Bake 20 minutes.

Tuna On A Muffin
(Serves 2)

1/2 can tuna, drained
2 tablespoons chopped celery
2 tablespoons chopped green or dry onion
1 tablespoon chopped dill pickle or 1/4 teaspoon dill
2 teaspoons prepared mustard
2 tablespoons mayonnaise
Dash salt and pepper
1 tablespoon grated cheddar cheese

Mix all ingredients except cheese. Spoon on English muffins and sprinkle with cheese. Broil until cheese melts.

Tuna Loaf
(Serves 1 generously)

Protein-rich, low in fat, and inexpensive, this loaf recipe was developed by Jacquelyn Bee, an energetic 82-year-old. She serves it with lemon wedges, green beans, and a mixed fruit salad.

1/2 cup water-packed tuna, drained
2 tablespoons dry bread crumbs
1 egg, slightly beaten
1 tablespoon oats
2 tablespoons skim or low-fat milk
1 tablespoon lemon juice
1 tablespoon chopped parsley
1 tablespoon chopped green onion (scallion)
1 tablespoon chopped olives
1/4 teaspoon salt
Dash pepper
3 tablespoons soft bread crumbs

Preheat oven to 400°. Mix all ingredients except soft bread crumbs. Spoon into oiled loaf pan. Bake for 20 minutes. Sprinkle soft crumbs over loaf and return to oven for 5 minutes to brown, or brown under broiler.

Liquids are Important
Most people know the value of fiber in the diet, but many are not aware that with increased fiber, we need more liquids. Drink water at mealtimes and during the day — at least 8 to 10 cups. Serve more than coffee with meals: bouillon, vegetable juice, fruit juice and clear soup are good choices. Plenty of non-alcoholic liquid intake will help prevent dehydration, constipation and illness.

Tuna au Gratin
(Serves 2)

1 7-ounce can tuna, drained
4 tablespoons chopped onion
2 tablespoons chopped green pepper
3 tablespoons mayonnaise
1 teaspoon lemon juice
2 tablespoons dry bread or cracker crumbs
2 tablespoons grated Parmesan or other cheese

Preheat oven to 350°. Mix all ingredients except crumbs and cheese. Spoon into baking dish. Top with crumbs and cheese. Bake 20 minutes.

Shrimp-Corn Curry
(Serves 2)

1/2 cup small cooked shrimp, canned or fresh
1 cup cooked corn
1/2 cup chopped celery
1/2 teaspoon curry powder
1 1/2 tablespoons mayonnaise
Dash salt and pepper
Lettuce

Mix curry powder and mayonnaise. Stir in all other ingredients except lettuce. Salt and pepper to taste. Place in refrigerator to chill. Serve on bed of chopped lettuce.

NOTE: Many physicians recommend limiting the consumption of eggs to 2 or 3 per week. Consult your doctor if you need to restrict your dietary intake of fats and/or cholesterol.

Eggs & Cheese

Macaroni and Cheese
Onion-Pepper Omelet
Tomato-Egg Bake
Swiss Eggs
Yogurt and Egg Dressing
Dr. B's Cheese Enchiladas
Broccoli and Egg
Double Cheese
Cheese Soubise
Bacon and Potato Eggs
Chili Cheese
Corn Pudding
ElRose's Bacon and Eggs
Egg Foo Yung
Eggs Benedict
Easy Hollandaise Sauce
Not-Quite Quiche
Cheese Pudding
Eggs with Corn and Bacon
Egg-in-a-Nest
Mushroom-Zucchini Frittata

Macaroni and Cheese
(Serves 2)

A rich, creamy, cheesy version of an old favorite. To add even more protein, stir in cubes of cooked chicken, turkey or ham or sliced frankfurters. For lower sodium content, use chicken or turkey, low-sodium cheese, and no additional salt.

> 1 cup cooked macaroni noodles
> 1 tablespoon butter or margarine
> 1 tablespoon flour
> 1 teaspoon dry mustard
> Dash hot pepper sauce
> 1/4 teaspoon salt
> 1 cup milk
> 1 cup grated cheddar cheese

Preheat oven to 375°. Melt butter in saucepan. Stir in flour, mustard and salt and heat until bubbly. Add milk and cook, stirring, until slightly thickened. Remove from heat and stir in 3/4 cup cheese and hot pepper sauce. Add macaroni and stir. Spoon into greased baking dish and sprinkle with remaining cheese. Bake 20 minutes.

Calcium in Your Diet
Dairy products are a good source of calcium, but they may not give all you need. If your doctor suggests calcium supplements, ask about the best quantity for you. Megadoses of calcium can increase the risk of kidney stones.

Onion-Pepper Omelet
(Serves 1)

1/4 onion, sliced thin
1/4 green bell pepper, sliced thin
2 teaspoons vegetable oil
2 eggs
1/8 teaspoon nutmeg
1/8 teaspoon sweet basil
Dash dill, salt and pepper

Heat oil in skillet. Sauté onion and pepper slices, stirring, until onion is golden brown. Beat eggs lightly with fork or whisk and add seasonings. Pour into skillet and cook over medium heat until eggs are set. Lift edges occasionally to allow uncooked portion to pour into bottom of pan. With spatula, fold omelet in half. Garnish with parsley.

Tomato-Egg Bake
(Serves 1)

1 large, fresh tomato
1 egg
1/4 teaspoon dill
1 teaspoon chopped onion
1 tablespoon grated cheese

Preheat oven to 350°. Slice top off tomato and scoop out pulp, leaving a thick shell. Mix tomato pulp with egg and all other ingredients. Stuff tomato shell with mixture. Place in buttered baking dish and bake 15-20 minutes, until egg sets. Top with additional grated cheese and return to oven to allow cheese to melt.

Swiss Eggs
(Serves 1)

1 hardcooked egg, sliced
1 tablespoon butter or margarine
2 teaspoons flour
3/4 cup milk
1/4 cup grated Swiss cheese
1/4 teaspoon dry mustard
1 tablespoon sherry wine (optional)
1 slice toast

Preheat oven to 350°. Melt butter in saucepan. Stir in flour and heat until bubbly. Slowly add milk, stirring until smooth. Add mustard and 2 tablespoons cheese. Add sherry. Tear toast into bite-sized pieces and place in buttered baking dish. Place egg slices on toast, pour sauce over and sprinkle with remaining cheese. Bake 10 minutes.

Yogurt and Egg Dressing
(About 2/3 cup)

This is a mixture that will add zest and protein to any crunchy green salad. It's low in fat and sodium.

1/2 cup plain, low-fat yogurt
1 hardcooked egg, chopped
1 teaspoon curry powder
1 green onion, chopped
Dash pepper

Mix all ingredients and chill.

Dr. B's Cheese Enchiladas
(Serves 3 - 4)

Dr. Steven Bailey, an Oregon naturopath, favors this dish for its great flavor combination and hints of Mexico. The recipe is easily doubled for serving a larger group.

    1 cup cheddar cheese
    1 cup Monterey jack cheese
    1/2 cup diced olives (small can)
    1/4 cup diced chiles
    1/2 onion, diced
    1 cup cottage cheese
    1/2 cup yogurt
    6 corn tortillas
    1 10-ounce can enchilada sauce

Preheat oven to 350°. Grate hard cheeses. Add all other ingredients except tortillas and enchilada sauce, and blend well. Set aside. In a skillet, heat 1/2 can of enchilada sauce with a little water to thin and a few drops of oil to prevent scorching. One at a time, heat tortillas in sauce (a few seconds each side) to soften. Stack softened tortillas in casserole dish. Place 1/4 cup cheese mixture in each tortilla. Roll tortillas, arranging in casserole. Pour other half of can of enchilada sauce over tortillas. Bake 20-25 minutes.

Freeze Extra Eggs
If you have more fresh eggs than you will use within ten days or so, break them into a glass or plastic container and place them in the freezer. They will keep for several weeks. (Don't try to freeze eggs in the shell.)

Broccoli and Egg
(Serves 1)

2 teaspoons vegetable oil
1/2 cup chopped fresh broccoli
1/4 cup water
1 egg
Dash salt and pepper
1/4 teaspoon sweet basil
Pinch marjoram
2 tablespoons milk.

Heat oil in skillet. Add broccoli and cook, stirring, for 1 minute. Add water, cover and simmer for 5 minutes. Remove pan from heat. Drain broccoli. Mix egg with all other ingredients. Pour egg mixture over broccoli and cook over low heat until egg is set — about 4 minutes.

Double Cheese
(Serves 1)
Soft, cheesy, rich and tasty.

1 egg
1 green onion, chopped
Dash salt and pepper
1/4 cup creamed small-curd cottage cheese
2 tablespoons grated cheddar cheese

Preheat oven to 350°. Mix all ingredients. Pour into buttered baking dish. Bake 20 minutes.

Cheese Soubise
(Serves 2)

A delicious version of a French country dish. It's a good use for leftover rice.

2 tablespoons butter or margarine
1/2 onion or 2 shallots, sliced
2 tablespoons chopped green bell pepper
1 cup cooked rice
1/2 cup chicken broth or bouillon
Dash salt and pepper
1/4 cup grated cheese

Preheat oven to 325°. Melt butter in skillet. Sauté onion and green pepper in butter until lightly browned. Stir in rice, salt, pepper and broth. Spoon into buttered baking dish and cover. Bake 40 minutes. Add cheese and stir to melt.

Bacon and Potato Eggs
(Serves 2)

1 potato, cooked and sliced
2 slices bacon
2 eggs
1 tablespoon milk
1/4 teaspoon Mixed Herbs
1/4 cup chopped tomatoes

Fry bacon in skillet until crisp. Add potato slices and fry until lightly browned. Mix eggs, milk, herbs and tomatoes in a bowl. Pour over potatoes and bacon. Cook over low heat until eggs are set.

Chili Cheese
(Serves 2)

This is a down-home favorite among those who like a spicy touch of Texas in their chili.

    1 slice bacon
    3 tablespoons chopped onion
    3 tablespoons chopped green or red bell pepper
    1/2 cup cooked kidney beans
    1/3 cup grated cheddar cheese
    1 fresh tomato, chopped, or 1/4 cup tomato sauce
    1/4 teaspoon chili powder or Mixed Hot Spices

Fry bacon until crisp, remove from skillet and crumble. Sauté onion and pepper in bacon fat. Add all other ingredients and bacon. Cook, stirring, 5 minutes.

Corn Pudding
(Serves 2)

    2 eggs, beaten
    1 cup cooked or canned corn, drained
    1 cup milk
    Dash salt
    Dash hot pepper sauce
    2 tablespoons chopped green onion
    1 celery stalk, chopped
    1 tablespoon chopped green pepper

Preheat oven to 350°. Mix corn, eggs and milk. Add remaining ingredients and mix. Pour into buttered baking dish. Set dish in hot water in shallow pan. Bake 40 minutes, until knife inserted in center comes out clean. Let stand 5 minutes to set before serving.

ElRose's Bacon and Eggs
(Serves 1)

ElRose Groves, hospitable hostess, served this quick and tasty dish often to her Bed-and-Breakfast guests.

1 slice bacon, cooked until almost crisp.
1 egg
2 tablespoons cottage cheese
Dash salt and pepper

Preheat oven to 350°. Place partially cooked bacon to form a circle around inside edge of custard cup or other small baking dish. Break egg into dish. Sprinkle with salt and pepper. Spoon cottage cheese over egg. Place in oven and bake 10 minutes or until egg is done as desired. Serve with dash of paprika and parsley sprig for color.

Egg Foo Yung
(Serves 2)

1 tablespoon vegetable oil
1/4 cup chopped onion
2 tablespoons chopped celery
1 clove garlic, chopped or pressed
1/2 cup chopped cooked shrimp, pork or chicken
2 tablespoons bean sprouts or chopped water chestnuts
3 eggs, lightly beaten
1 teaspoon soy sauce

Heat oil in skillet. Sauté onion and celery in oil until tender but crisp. Add garlic, shrimp and sprouts and stir. Mix eggs and soy sauce and pour over. When eggs are set, flip or fold in half, omelet-style.

Eggs Benedict
(Serves 1)

This gourmet treat is as easy as stacking a sandwich.

English muffin, toasted
Bacon slice, cooked and crumbled
Egg poached in milk
Hollandaise sauce, canned or homemade (see below)

Place bacon and egg on muffin. Pour warm sauce over and serve.

Easy Hollandaise Sauce

1 egg yolk
1 tablespoon lemon juice
Pinch salt
2 tablespoons butter or margarine

Blend egg yolk, lemon juice and salt. Melt butter in saucepan until bubbly. Slowly pour egg and lemon mixture into hot butter, stirring constantly.

Substitute Ingredients
Substitutes may be used for many ingredients in our recipes. Instead of egg, use frozen egg substitute; instead of yogurt, sour cream or sour cream substitute.

Not-Quite Quiche
(Serves 1)

It's easier to prepare than the real, traditional quiche, but it's full of similar rich goodness.

1 slice toast, broken into bite-sized pieces
1 tomato, peeled and sliced
2 slices bacon, cooked and crumbled (optional)
1/2 cup grated Swiss or cheddar cheese
1/2 cup milk
1 egg
Pinch salt and pepper
Dash hot pepper sauce
1/4 teaspoon prepared mustard

Preheat oven to 350°. Place toast pieces in small pie pan or baking dish. Add tomato slices and bacon. Sprinkle with grated cheese. Mix eggs, milk and seasonings and pour over other ingredients. Bake 30 minutes.

No-Fat Cooking
To avoid using fats in cooking, spray the skillet or baking dish with a non-stick commercial spray when your recipe calls for a greased pan. Or use pans that have been treated with non-stick coating.

Cheese Pudding
(Serves 1)

1 slice bread cut in cubes
1/3 cup Swiss or cheddar cheese cut in cubes
1/4 cup milk
1 egg
Dash hot pepper sauce
Salt and pepper
Dill

Preheat oven to 350°. Place bread and cheese in buttered baking dish. Combine milk, egg and hot pepper sauce in bowl and beat with fork until well blended. Pour milk and egg mixture over bread and cheese. Sprinkle with salt, pepper and dill. Bake 20 minutes, until puffy.

Eggs with Corn and Bacon
(Serves 2)

This mixture of eggs and vegetables is both creamy and crunchy.
2 slices bacon
1/2 onion, chopped
1/2 green bell pepper or other mild pepper, chopped
1/2 cup creamed corn
Dash salt and pepper
Dash hot pepper sauce
2 eggs, beaten

Fry bacon until crisp, remove from skillet, and crumble. Pour off bacon fat, leaving 1 tablespoon in skillet. Sauté onion and green pepper in bacon fat until tender. Add all other ingredients and cook over medium heat until eggs are set. Sprinkle crumbled bacon over eggs and serve.

Egg-in-a-Nest
(Serves 1)

Margaret Hoffman serves this, along with sliced oranges topped with powdered sugar, to her grandchildren when they come for a visit. The kids like to help by cutting the holes in the bread and, when they're old enough, cracking the egg into its "nest."

> 2 teaspoons butter or margarine
> 1 slice whole wheat bread
> 1 egg
> Dash salt and pepper
> Pinch sweet basil or dill

With knife or cookie cutter, cut hole in bread. Melt butter in skillet. Place bread on hot butter in skillet. Break egg into hole in bread. Sauté until light brown and turn. Continue cooking to taste. Sprinkle with salt, pepper and herbs.

Think Zinc
Zinc is a mineral that is often inadequate in our diets. It's essential for many metabolic processes and helps us resist disease and infection. Meat, seafood and eggs are good sources of zinc.

Mushroom-Zucchini Frittata
(Serves 2)

1/4 cup chopped fresh or canned mushrooms
2 tablespoons chopped onion
1/4 cup chopped zucchini
2 tablespoons vegetable oil
1 clove garlic, pressed or minced
3 eggs
1/4 cup milk or cream
Dash salt and pepper
1/2 cup soft bread crumbs
1/2 cup grated cheddar cheese

Preheat oven to 350°. Heat oil in skillet. Sauté mushrooms, onion and zucchini in oil until golden brown. Add garlic and stir. Beat eggs with milk or cream, salt and pepper. Add mushroom mixture, bread crumbs and cheese to eggs. Pour into baking dish or oven-proof skillet. Bake 30 minutes, until set in center and lightly browned.

Enjoy Every Mouthful
Eating well involves more than providing fuel for your body. It's a sensory experience that's meant to be savored. Eat slowly, taking the time to appreciate and enjoy your meal.

Soups

Corn Chowder

Creamy Tomato Soup

Mildred's Tomato-Cheese Soup

Moon's Minestrone

French Onion Soup

Summer Soup

Aunt Kathy's "You Ought To Start A Restaurant" Soup

Potato-Onion Soup

Lentil Soup

Salsa Soup

Penny's Thousand-Year Chicken Soup

Corn Chowder
(Serves 2, with leftovers)
Creamy and delicious with rich corn flavor.

2 tablespoons vegetable oil
1 tablespoon chopped onion
1 celery stalk
2 tablespoons flour
Dash pepper
1 chicken bouillon cube or 1/4 cup chicken broth
1/4 cup water if not using broth
1 cup milk
1 medium cooked potato, chopped
Pinch salt
1 small can creamed corn
Chopped parsley

Heat oil in saucepan. Sauté onion and celery in oil. Stir in flour and pepper and heat until bubbly. Dissolve bouillon cube in water if not using broth. Stir water or broth into flour mixture. Add milk and stir over medium heat until thickened. Add potato and creamed corn and simmer 2-3 minutes. If chowder is too thick, add milk to thin. Sprinkle each serving with parsley.

Grow and Snip Your Own
Fresh herbs add sparkle and verve to your meals, and the best way to get them is to grow your own. If you don't have outdoor space, grow chives, marjoram and thyme in pots on your kitchen windowsill. (Don't overwater, or they'll be spindly.) When you want a spoonful, all you do is snip!

Creamy Tomato Soup
(Serves 2)

A low-sodium special that costs little and is simple to prepare and home-made delicious.

> 1 tablespoon butter or margarine
> 1 tablespoon flour
> Dash pepper
> 1/4 teaspoon dill
> 1/4 teaspoon marjoram
> 1 cup milk
> 1/2 cup tomato sauce
> Several drops Tabasco or other hot pepper sauce

Melt butter in saucepan. Add flour and pepper, stirring until flour bubbles. Add milk and cook until thickened, stirring constantly with whisk. Add all other ingredients and stir until smooth. Heat but do not boil.

Mildred's Tomato-Cheese Soup
(Serves 1)

Mildred Waters, an artist from Laguna Beach, California, and active in her 90s, often prepares this nutritious soup for a light supper.

> 1/2 cup stewed tomatoes
> 2 tablespoons Swiss or cheddar cheese, grated
> 1 egg

Place tomatoes in saucepan, bring to boil and simmer to reduce liquid. Add cheese. Beat egg slightly and stir into tomato-cheese mixture. Serve hot with buttered toast.

Moon's Minestrone
(Serves 6-8)

A university professor, "Moon" often shared this favorite recipe with his students. He advised cooking "lots of soup; it's good the next day and easy to freeze for later."

4 cups water
1 1/2 pounds beef with bone (or stew meat)
1/4 cup kidney beans
1/2 teaspoon salt
2 bay leaves
1/4 cup chopped celery
1 onion, sliced
1/2 teaspoon hot pepper sauce
1 16-ounce can tomatoes
1 cup shredded cabbage
3 carrots, sliced
1/2 cup vermicelli pasta
1 cup frozen peas
1 zucchini, sliced
Parmesan cheese, grated

Combine water, beef, beans, salt and bay leaves in kettle. Heat to boiling and skim foam. Cover and simmer 2 hours. Add celery, onion, hot sauce, cabbage, tomatoes and carrots and simmer 30 minutes. Add vermicelli, peas and zucchini and simmer 15 minutes. Remove bay leaves and serve, topped with Parmesan cheese.

French Onion Soup
(Serves 1)

4 tablespoons dried onion soup mix
1/4 onion, sliced
2 teaspoons vegetable oil
Thick slice French bread
2 tablespoons grated Parmesan cheese

Prepare soup according to package directions, using 1 cup water. Heat oil in skillet. Sauté onion slices in oil. Add soup to skillet and simmer. Place French bread in soup bowl and ladle soup over it. Sprinkle with cheese. Place under broiler a few seconds to melt cheese.

Summer Soup
(Serves 2)

A chilled vegetable soup, perfect for a hot summer evening.

1 tablespoon butter or margarine or vegetable oil
1 cup chopped broccoli
2 cups chicken or vegetable broth
1/2 onion, chopped
1/4 teaspoon salt
Dash pepper
Dash nutmeg
1/4 teaspoon curry powder
1 teaspoon chopped parsley
1 tablespoon lemon juice

Heat oil or butter in skillet. Sauté onion until tender. Add all other ingredients except lemon juice. Simmer 10 minutes. Cool, then purée in blender or food processor. Add lemon juice and chill in refrigerator 4 hours or more.

Aunt Kathy's "You Ought To Start A Restaurant" Soup

(Serves 4, or 1 teenaged boy)

Kathy Newman, an Oregon teacher, served this to her teen-aged nephew Ben, and his response was, "You oughta start a restaurant!" Kathy serves the soup with a sprinkle of chopped cilantro and corn chips on the side.

> 1 15-ounce can tomato sauce
> 1 1/2 cups water or chicken broth
> 1 tablespoon butter
> 1 cup chopped vegetables (onion, carrot, celery, broccoli, zucchini)
> 1/2 15-ounce can garbanzo beans
> 1/2 15-ounce can black beans
> 1 cup dried spiral pasta
> 2 teaspoons ground cumin
> 1 teaspoon dried basil
> 1 garlic clove, minced
> Salt and pepper to taste

Melt butter in large saucepan. Sauté vegetables in butter until slightly softened, about 3-4 minutes. Add tomato sauce, broth or water, pasta and herbs. Simmer until pasta is tender. Stir in beans. Heat, add salt and pepper to taste, and serve.

Seek Variety

To maintain a balanced diet and fend off mealtime boredom, eat a variety of foods. Be adventurous and try a new flavor or dish or spice occasionally. Once you may have disliked yogurt or cayenne pepper or broccoli; but tastes change, and you may find new enjoyment that surprises you.

Potato-Onion Soup
(Serves 2)

Easy and quick to make with dried, packaged potatoes.

    1/2 cup water
    1/2 onion, chopped
    1 chicken bouillon cube
    1 cup low-fat or skim milk
    1/2 cup instant packaged mashed potatoes
    Dash salt
    Chopped parsley

Combine water, onion and bouillon in saucepan and heat to boiling. Stir in milk, instant potatoes and salt and heat. Thin with more milk if desired. Sprinkle with parsley and serve.

Lentil Soup
(Serves 2 generously)

A soup with hearty, robust goodness — perfect for a cold winter's night. Serve with a green salad and hot biscuits or French bread.

    1/2 cup uncooked lentils
    4 cups water
    1 pork or ham bone
    1/4 cup chopped celery
    1/4 cup chopped carrots
    2 tablespoons chopped onion
    Dash pepper

Place all ingredients in large saucepan. Bring to boil, turn down heat and simmer about 2 hours. Remove ham or pork bone, cut any meat from bone and place meat in soup. Season to taste.

Salsa Soup
Serves 1

Make this speedy, tasty soup as spicy or mild as you prefer, and serve it with tortilla chips or cornmeal muffins. Add cooked chopped chicken or shrimp to make a heartier dish.

    1 teaspoon vegetable oil
    1 chopped green onion or 1 tablespoon chopped
        yellow onion
    1 tablespoon chopped red bell pepper
    1 clove garlic, minced
    1/4 teaspoon cumin
    2/3 cup chicken or vegetable broth
    1/2 tomato, chopped
    1/2 celery stalk, chopped
    1 teaspoon lemon or lime juice
    1/4 teaspoon hot or mild chili pepper, chopped
    1 tablespoon chopped cilantro

Heat oil in saucepan. Sauté onion, red pepper and garlic 1 minute. Add cumin and stir. Add broth, tomato, celery and lime juice. Simmer 5 minutes. Ladle into bowl and top with cilantro.

Lemon, the Great Flavorizer
Many good cooks say their secret lies in that package of tangy flavor, the fresh lemon. Its juice and grated rind can enhance almost any dish, from meat loaf to oatmeal cookies. To make a lemon easier to squeeze, simmer the whole fruit in water for 5 minutes.

Penny's Thousand-Year Chicken Soup
(Serves 2 generously)

Penny Avila, a gifted poet, says she has been cooking this delicious soup for "a thousand years." Refrigerate or freeze the unused portion for another meal.

> Back and neck of chicken or turkey
> 2 whole onions, cut in chunks
> 2 stalks celery, cut in chunks
> 1 parsnip, chopped
> 1 turnip, chopped
> 2 carrots, sliced
> 1/2 teaspoon salt
> Water

Pull and discard fat and skin from poultry pieces. Place pieces in kettle and cover completely with water. Bring to a boil and skim off foam. Add all other ingredients. Simmer 3 hours. Discard bones before serving.

Almost-Free Soup
Save the bones of poultry, meat or fish in a plastic bag in the refrigerator (or freezer, if saving longer than 2 days). When you've collected a few odds and ends of vegetables — half an onion here, a zucchini or carrot there — throw them together with 3 cups of water, parsley sprigs, a bay leaf, a squeeze of lemon, a garlic clove and a dash of salt and pepper. Simmer for a couple of hours, discard the bones, and you'll have a nutritious, delicious meal that costs next to nothing.

Vegetables & Fruits

Potato Nachos

Norma's Classic Tomato Sandwich

Quick-Stuffed Baked Potato

Zucchini Linguine

Mashed Potatoes Plus

Vegetarian Gravy

Wilted Spinach with Garlic and Nuts

Green Beans Parmesan

Coleslaw with Pineapple and Carrots

Black Beans 'n Rice

Carrot-Raisin Salad

Waldorf Delight

Lentils and Rice

Chilled Bean Salad

Golden Salad

Classic Macaroni Salad

Minty Fruit Salad

Cranberry Pears

Peachy Banana Shake

Garden Stew

Ginger Carrots

Onions au Gratin

Carolyn's Ratatouille

Potatoes and Green Beans

Pineapple Beets

Vegetable-Rice

Pineapple-Carrots

Spanish Rice

Salad Faces

Apple-Carrot Slaw

Fried Rice

Nan's Cranberry Salad

House Salad

Shish-ka-bob Salad

Grated Carrot Salad

Baked Apple

Pineapple Smoothie

Frozen Banana

Potato Nachos
(Serves 1)

Most kids like nachos, a hot snack usually made with tortilla chips and cheese. Here's another version you can introduce to the grandchildren. They can help with spreading potato slices and sprinkling them with cheese.

> 1 potato, cut in 1/4-inch slices (peel if desired)
> 1/4 cup grated cheddar cheese

Preheat oven to 375°. Place potato slices in single layer on buttered baking sheet.. Bake 15 minutes. Turn potatoes and sprinkle with cheese. Bake 10 minutes.

Garden Stew
(Serves 2, with leftovers)

This meal-in-a-dish was a favorite of Eudora Benson, a retired bookkeeper too busy planning her next travel adventure to spend much time in the kitchen. "Just remember, it's a quarter-cup of everything," she said.

> 1/4 cup each:
> > chopped broccoli, fresh or frozen
> > grated cheddar cheese
> > chopped mushrooms, fresh or canned
> > evaporated milk
> > bacon, fried crisp and crumbled (2 slices)
> > chopped onion

Preheat oven to 350°. Place broccoli in buttered baking dish. Cover with cheese. Add bacon and mushrooms. Pour milk over all. Bake uncovered 20 minutes. Remove from oven, place onions on top, and bake 10 minutes more.

Norma's Classic Tomato Sandwich
(Serves 1)

Norma Huse shares this simple, classic recipe, which she got from her father and now fixes for her numerous grandchildren. It's a tomato-lover's favorite.

> 2 slices good-quality white bread, preferably homemade
> 1 half-inch slice garden ripened, red tomato, equal
>   to the width of the bread (best if it's
>   sun-warmed, fresh off the vine)
> Soft butter
> Salt
> Fresh ground black pepper
> "Irreverent additions" (optional): thinly sliced onion,
> crisp bacon, grated Grafton Village Reserve
> cheese, mayonnaise)

Spread butter on bread slices. Place tomato slice on buttered bread. Add salt and pepper to taste. Place bread slices together and enjoy.

Quick-Stuffed Baked Potato
(Serves 1)

> 1 medium potato, washed, unpeeled
> 1/4 cup cooked chili, with or without meat
> 3 tablespoons grated cheddar cheese

Preheat oven to 400°. Bake potato 50 - 60 minutes, until fork-tender. Heat chili in saucepan. Split potato; pour chili over. Top with cheese. Place potato on aluminum foil under broiler and broil until cheese melts.

Ginger Carrots
(Serves 1)

The gentle bite of ginger and garlic combines with the natural sweetness of vitamin-rich carrots for a pleasing vegetable dish.

> 1/2 carrot, cut in slivers
> 2 teaspoons butter or margarine
> 1/4 teaspoon chopped fresh ginger
> 1 clove garlic, chopped or pressed
> 1/4 cup white wine or water

Heat butter or margarine in skillet. Sauté carrot slivers until light golden-brown. Add ginger and garlic and stir (do not brown). Add wine or water, cover and simmer 5-8 minutes. Remove cover and simmer until liquid evaporates.

Onions au Gratin
(Serves 2)

Rich in flavor and distinctively spicy.

> 1/2 onion, chopped
> 1 tablespoon butter or margarine
> 2 tablespoons flour
> Dash salt and pepper
> Few drops hot pepper sauce
> 1/4 teaspoon ground cumin
> 1/2 cup grated cheese

Preheat oven to 350°. Heat butter in skillet. Sauté onions in butter until tender. Remove pan from heat. Stir in all other ingredients, reserving 2 tablespoons of cheese. Place mixture in greased baking dish or custard cups and sprinkle with reserved cheese. Bake uncovered 20 minutes.

Zucchini Linguine
(Serves 2)

Zucchini and other vegetables make this pasta dish nutritious and colorful. And it is quick to prepare.

> 2 green onions, chopped
> 2 teaspoons olive oil
> 1 medium zucchini, chopped
> 1 garlic clove, chopped
> 1/2 cup vegetable or chicken broth
> 1 stalk celery, chopped
> 1 tablespoon parsley, chopped
> 1 tablespoon fresh basil or 1/2 tablespoon dry
> 1/2 tablespoon lemon juice
> 1/4 teaspoon salt
> 1/8 teaspoon pepper
> 1 cup cooked linguine or other pasta
> Parmesan or other cheese, grated

Heat olive oil in skillet. Sauté onion until soft. Add zucchini and garlic and cook 5 minutes, stirring often. Add all other ingredients except pasta and simmer 5 minutes, stirring occasionally. Stir zucchini mixture into hot pasta and sprinkle with cheese of choice.

Contrast Aids Appetites
When you serve soft foods, such as mashed potatoes and gelatin salad, contrast them with crunchy ones like cucumbers and broccoli. Contrast colors, too, so your place will seem appealing. Foods come in so many colors, you can make your plate as colorful as an artist's palette — and that will please your palate.

Carolyn's Ratatouille
(Serves 8)

Carolyn Ostergren, a dietitian, makes a batch of this tasty vegetable stew and freezes part of it. After a busy day, all she has to do is heat it for a nutritious supper. It has only about 50 calories per cup.

1 eggplant, peeled and cut in 1/2-inch cubes
6 medium zucchini, peeled and sliced thickly
2 green or red bell peppers, seeded and cut in chunks
2 stalks celery, cut in diagonal slices
2 cloves garlic, minced
2-3 tablespoons chopped parsley
1/4 teaspoon pepper
1 teaspoon oregano
2 tablespoons vinegar
Dash hot pepper sauce
6 cups diced, canned tomatoes
2 cups chopped fresh mushrooms

In soup kettle, combine all ingredients except mushrooms. Cover, bring to a boil, and simmer over low heat 20 minutes. Remove cover and cook over moderate heat 15 more minutes, stirring to prevent scorching. Add mushrooms, heat and serve.

More Flavor, Not Less

Contrary to popular belief, older people do not usually need bland diets with fewer seasonings. The opposite is true; as our taste buds become less sensitive with age, we need more flavor-enhancing, not less. Experiment with herbs and spices to find combinations that lend zest to the foods you eat.

Mashed Potatoes Plus
(Serves 2)

A soufflé-like dish that's full of dairy goodness. With a crisp green vegetable or salad, it makes a meal.

1/2 cup hot mashed potato (1 cooked potato or
      1/3 cup instant packaged potato)
1/4 cup milk
1/4 teaspoon salt
2 teaspoons butter, melted
1 egg, separated
1 tablespoon lemon juice
2 tablespoons grated cheddar or Swiss cheese

Preheat oven to 375°. Mix milk, salt, butter and egg yolks with mashed potato. In a separate bowl, beat egg white until stiff peaks form. Fold white into potato mixture. Stir in lemon juice. Place in buttered baking dish and top with cheese. Bake 20 minutes.

Potatoes and Green Beans
(Serves 1)

1/2 potato, sliced
1/4 cup fresh green beans, chopped
1 teaspoon butter or margarine
1/2 teaspoon dill
Dash salt
1 tablespoon grated cheddar cheese

Place potato slices in saucepan. Place beans on potatoes. Add water to cover. Cover pan, bring to boil and simmer 10 minutes. Drain and add all other ingredients. Cover and remove from heat. Serve when cheese has melted.

Vegetarian Gravy
(Makes 2 cups)

Dr. Steven Bailey, a naturopathic physician and a vegetarian, provided this recipe for a delicious meatless gravy. He prepares it for family holiday dinners and says there is never a spoonful left. It's good served on rice, pasta, or cooked grains.

2 tablespoons olive oil
1 yellow onion, diced
2 cloves garlic, chopped
4-6 fresh mushrooms, chopped
2 tablespoons flour
1 soup packet (2 tablespoons) Edward & Sons'
     "Miso-Cup"
1 tablespoon butter
1/2 cup red wine
1 cup water

Heat oil in skillet. Sauté onions, garlic and mushrooms in oil until softened and lightly browned. Set aside. Place flour in clean dry skillet and heat until light brown, stirring. Do not allow to burn. Add Miso-Cup powder and butter to flour and cook, stirring, for 1 minute. Add wine and water and cook, stirring, until blended and thickened. Stir in onion mixture. Add water if gravy is too thick.

Pep Up Your Appetite
Pay attention to how food looks, just as you do with guests. A parsley garnish or a curl of orange peel adds to the attractive appearance of your meal. It will taste better if it looks good to eat.

Pineapple Beets
(Serves 2)

1/3 cup canned pineapple chunks, drained
3 tablespoons liquid from drained pineapple
1 tablespoon vinegar
3/4 teaspoon cornstarch
1/4 teaspoon Mixed Sweet Spices
1 cup (1 small can) sliced beets, drained

Place all ingredients except pineapple chunks and beets in saucepan and mix well. Simmer, stirring, until thickened. Add beets and pineapple and heat.

Vegetable-Rice
(Serves 2)

1 tablespoon vegetable oil and 1 teaspoon butter
1/2 potato, diced (peel if preferred)
1/2 carrot, diced (peel if preferred)
1/3 cup fresh chopped green beans or 4 tablespoons
        frozen beans
1/4 cup uncooked rice, brown or white
1/4 teaspoon Mixed Hot Spices
1 clove garlic, minced or pressed
1/8 teaspoon minced fresh ginger
1 cup chicken broth or bouillon

Heat oil in saucepan. Add potato, carrot and beans and sauté, stirring, 1 minute. Add all other ingredients except broth and cook 2 minutes. Add broth and bring to boil. Cover and simmer 20 minutes for white rice, 40 minutes for brown rice.

Wilted Spinach with Garlic and Nuts
(Serves 1)

A delicious vegetable dish that takes only moments to prepare.

> 1 teaspoon olive oil or vegetable oil
> 2 cloves garlic, chopped
> 1 cup fresh, washed spinach, chopped
> 1 tablespoon toasted walnuts (or pecans or pine nuts)
> Dash salt and pepper
> Lemon juice

Heat oil in skillet. Sauté garlic in oil for a few seconds, until light golden brown. Remove garlic; set aside. Place spinach in skillet and cook over medium heat, stirring until spinach wilts. Add garlic, nuts, salt and pepper. Serve with a sprinkle of lemon juice.

Green Beans Parmesan
(Serves 2)

Parmesan cheese dresses up an ordinary green vegetable and turns it into party fare.

> 1 tablespoon butter or margarine
> 1 tablespoon chopped onion
> 1/2 cup green beans, fresh or frozen
> 3 tablespoons water
> Pinch salt
> 1/4 teaspoon sweet basil, fresh or dried
> 3 tablespoons grated Parmesan cheese

Heat butter in saucepan. Sauté onion in butter until lightly browned. Add all other ingredients except cheese. Cover and simmer until tender, about 10-12 minutes. Sprinkle with cheese.

Pineapple-Carrots
(Serves 1)

1/2 carrot, minced
2 tablespoons crushed pineapple, drained
1 teaspoon butter or margarine
Dash salt
1 tablespoon rum (optional)
1/4 teaspoon Mixed Sweet Spices

Preheat oven to 350°. Simmer carrots in saucepan with 1/4 cup water 5 minutes. Place carrots and all other ingredients in buttered baking dish. Bake 10 minutes.

Spanish Rice
(Serves 1)

2 teaspoons vegetable oil
2 tablespoons chopped green bell pepper
2 tablespoons chopped onion
1 clove garlic, minced
1/4 teaspoon dried sweet basil
1/4 cup uncooked white or brown rice
1/4 cup chopped tomato, fresh or canned
1/8 teaspoon salt
1/8 teaspoon oregano
Dash pepper
1/2 cup water

Heat oil in skillet. Sauté green pepper and onion in oil until tender. Add garlic and basil and stir. Add all other ingredients and cover. Simmer 20 minutes for white rice and 40-45 minutes for brown rice.

Coleslaw with Pineapple and Carrots
(Serves 2)

1/2 cup grated cabbage
1/4 cup grated carrot
1/4 cup canned crushed pineapple or chunk pineapple
1 tablespoon mayonnaise
1 teaspoon lemon juice
1 tablespoon liquid from canned pineapple

Mix all ingredients. Chill and serve.

Black Beans 'n Rice
(Serves 2)

Nutritious beans, brown rice and vegetables combine with hot spices to create a delicious dish that's good on its own or as a tortilla filling. Top it with salsa for extra zing.

1 teaspoon olive oil
1/2 onion, chopped
1 clove garlic, minced
1 tablespoon chopped green pepper, hot or mild
1/4 cup grated carrot
1/3 cup brown rice
1 cup water or vegetable or chicken broth
1/2 teaspoon Mixed Hot Spices
Dash hot pepper sauce
1 cup black beans, canned or dried and cooked
1 teaspoon lime or lemon juice

Heat oil in skillet. Sauté onion, garlic, rice, pepper and carrot in oil, until onion softens. Stir in spices and hot sauce. Add water or broth, cover and steam for 30 minutes, until rice is tender. Add beans and lime or lemon juice and heat.

Salad Faces
(Serves 2)

Even kids who refuse to eat vegetables find this one interesting. Use your imagination (or theirs) and you'll think of more ways to embellish it (broccoli or mayonnaise beard, celery stick mustache, cauliflower ears . . .).

    2 thick slices of a fresh tomato
    1/2 carrot cut in rounds
    1 radish cut in half
    1 teaspoon currants or 1 thin slice green pepper
    Parsley sprigs
    Lettuce

Place tomato slices on lettuce on salad plates. Make faces using carrot rounds for eyes, radish halves for noses, currants or green pepper as mouths, and parsley for hair.

Carrot-Raisin Salad
(Serves 1)

    1 small carrot, grated
    3 tablespoons raisins
    1/4 teaspoon fresh ginger, chopped
    2 teaspoons plain, low-fat yogurt
    Dash nutmeg
    Lettuce

To plump raisins, cover with water in saucepan and bring to boil. Remove from heat and set aside 5 minutes, then drain. Mix all ingredients and chill. Serve on bed of chopped lettuce.

Apple-Carrot Slaw
(Serves 2)

1/2 cup shredded cabbage
2 tablespoons grated carrots
1/4 cup nuts, chopped
1/2 apple, chopped
2 tablespoons raisins
Dressing
2 tablespoons yogurt
1/4 cup cottage cheese
2 tablespoons apple juice

Mix all ingredients except dressing. Place dressing ingredients in blender or food processor and mix until smooth. Pour dressing over mixed salad.

Waldorf Delight
(Serves 1)

1/2 medium apple, chopped
1 teaspoon lemon juice
1 celery stalk, chopped
1 tablespoon chopped walnuts
2 teaspoons mayonnaise
2 tablespoons yogurt
1 teaspoon honey
Lettuce

Sprinkle apple slices with lemon juice and drizzle with honey. Add all other ingredients except lettuce and mix well. Serve on bed of chopped lettuce.

Fried Rice
(Serves 2)

1 tablespoon vegetable oil
1 tablespoon chopped onion
1 tablespoon chopped green bell pepper
1/2 cup cooked rice
2 tablespoons chopped, canned water chestnuts (optional)
3 mushrooms, sliced
2 teaspoons soy sauce
1 egg, lightly beaten

Heat oil in skillet. Sauté onion, green pepper and mushrooms in oil until tender but crisp. Add rice, water chestnuts and soy sauce. Cook 5 minutes, stirring often. Add egg. Cook 3 minutes, stirring constantly.

Lentils and Rice
(Serves 2)

1/4 cup chopped onion
1/2 cup cooked brown rice
1/2 cup cooked lentils
1 egg, slightly beaten
1/4 teaspoon salt
1 clove garlic, minced
1/2 cup dry bread cubes
1/2 cup canned tomatoes
1/2 teaspoon Mixed Hot Spices

Preheat oven to 350°. Mix all ingredients and pour into oiled baking dish. Bake 30 minutes. Serve with catsup or sauce of heated, condensed cream soup.

Nan's Cranberry Salad
(Serves 8 - 10)

Nan Narboe, a former restaurant owner, likes to prepare this crunchy, fruit-filled molded salad during the winter holidays. Because it's a homemade version of the traditional gelatin mold, it takes more time to make, but the effort is well worth it.

> 2 envelopes unflavored gelatin
> 1/2 cup water
> 1 1/2 cups chilled water
> 2 tablespoons white grape juice concentrate or
>   1/4 cup honey
> 1 cup frozen raspberry or cranberry-raspberry
>   juice concentrate
> 1 package (about 2 cups) uncooked cranberries,
>   fresh or frozen, rinsed and picked over.
> 1 orange, peeled
> 1 firm but not tart apple, peeled and grated
> 1 cup diced celery
> 1/2 cup toasted walnuts, chopped (optional)

Pour gelatin and 1/2 cup water into small saucepan and allow gelatin to soften. Heat until gelatin melts. Add honey or grape juice concentrate to gelatin, stir, remove from heat, and pour into mixing bowl. Add raspberry concentrate and stir. Add chilled water to mixture. Place in refrigerator to chill until mixture turns syrupy and begins to jell. Check often, as it thickens quickly (usually less than an hour, if water is ice-cold). Slice orange and remove seeds. Chop cranberries and orange slices in food processor or blender. When gelatin is thickened but not firm, mix in all chopped ingredients. Chill until firm.

Chilled Bean Salad
(Serves 2)

1/2 cup cold cooked green beans, canned or fresh
1/4 red onion, sliced thin
1/4 cup sliced mushrooms, fresh or canned
2 tablespoons vegetable oil
2 tablespoons vinegar

Dressing
2 tablespoons plain yogurt
1 tablespoon mayonnaise
1 clove garlic, pressed or minced
1/4 teaspoon dill weed
1/4 teaspoon lemon juice
1/8 teaspoon dry mustard

Mix all ingredients except dressing. Cover and marinate overnight. Mix dressing ingredients and chill. Drain marinated salad, pour dressing over and serve on lettuce.

Emergency Planning
Be prepared for bad weather or days when you're unable to get to the grocery store. Stock an emergency shelf with nonfat instant powdered milk, peanut butter, canned soups and fruits, canned fish and stews. If you have a freezer, keep a week's supply of meat, bread and vegetables on hand. Cheese and milk may also be frozen.

House Salad

The grandchildren will love helping construct this one. It's as much fun as making a candy house, and a lot more nutritious.

    4 celery stalks, cut in thirds
    Peanut butter
    Cucumber, sliced lengthwise
    Radishes, sliced
    Carrot stick
    Broccoli flowerets
    Lettuce

Fill celery stalks with peanut butter and stack them like logs to make 3 walls, 4 celery stalks high. For 4th wall, place smaller celery pieces vertically, leaving an opening as a doorway. Stand a carrot stick as a chimney. Make an angled roof with cucumber slices and secure with toothpicks. Peanut butter on the edges helps the slices stick. Use radish slices as windows, securing with a dab of peanut butter. Place broccoli around the house as trees and shrubs and lettuce shreds as grass. Make a person out of a carrot stick and a radish slice, securing with toothpicks. Use your imagination to create more.

Vitamin A: Good and Bad

Vitamin A is necessary to good health — but don't overdo it. An excess of Vitamin A can cause numerous problems. Your doctor or dietitian may suggest beta-carotene as a safer supplement. Daily servings of yellow and leafy green vegetables may supply all the Vitamin A your body needs.

Golden Salad
(Serves 1)

1/2 carrot, grated
1/2 orange, cut in sections
1/2 teaspoon grated orange rind
Chopped lettuce

Dressing
    1 teaspoon honey
    2 teaspoons vinegar
    1/2 teaspoon soy sauce
    2 teaspoons vegetable oil

Place carrot, orange and rind on lettuce. Mix dressing ingredients and pour over.

Shish-ka-bob Salad

Here's a salad that is fun to prepare with the grandchildren. With the ingredients cut and ready to go, young fingers can thread them on to skewers according to taste. It works well with fruits, too.

Skewers
Cucumber, cut in chunks
Radishes
Cherry tomatoes
Mushrooms, halved
Green or red bell pepper, cut in chunks
Celery chunks
Cubes of cheddar, Swiss or other hard cheese

Spear vegetables and cheeses on skewers, shish-ka-bob style, and serve.

Classic Macaroni Salad
(Serves 2 generously)

From Vera Porter's recipe file comes this old favorite, a salad both smooth and crunchy, ideal for a summer supper.

1/3 cup mayonnaise
1 tablespoon vinegar
2 teaspoons prepared mustard
1/2 teaspoon sugar
1/2 teaspoon salt
1/8 teaspoon pepper
4 ounces elbow macaroni, cooked and drained
1/2 cup chopped celery
1/2 cup chopped green or red bell pepper
2 tablespoons chopped onion

Mix together mayonnaise, vinegar and seasonings. Add remaining ingredients and toss to coat well.

Grated Carrot Salad
(Serves 1)

1/2 carrot, grated
1/4 cup grated zucchini
2 tablespoons walnuts or cashews (optional)
1 teaspoon honey
2 teaspoons vinegar
1/2 teaspoon soy sauce
2 teaspoons vegetable oil

Combine all ingredients and mix well.

Minty Fruit Salad
(Serves 1)

Banana, orange, grapefruit, pear, melon, or other fruits
(fresh, frozen or canned)
3 - 4 mint leaves, fresh or dried
1 tablespoon lemon juice
2 tablespoons plain yogurt

Chop fruit to equal 1 cup. Mix fruit with mint and lemon juice.
Allow to stand 15 minutes. Top with yogurt and garnish with mint
leaf.

Baked Apple
(Serves 1)

1 apple
1 tablespoon brown sugar
1 teaspoon butter or margarine
1/4 teaspoon cinnamon
1 teaspoon raisins

Preheat oven to 400°. Core apple (or cut in half and scoop out
core from each half). Place apple or apple halves in baking dish
and fill with sugar, butter, cinnamon and raisins. Cover bottom of
pan with water, 1/4 inch deep. Bake 30 minutes or until tender
when pierced with fork.

Chewing Solutions
*Avoid chewy sweets, berries, nuts and other foods that stick
easily in teeth. When nuts are called for in the recipes in this
book, they are almost always optional.*

Cranberry Pears
(Serves 1)

1 fresh whole pear
1/4 cup cranberry sauce
1 tablespoon lemon juice
Dash allspice

Preheat oven to 350°. Stand pear in baking dish. Mix lemon, cranberry sauce and allspice and spoon over pear. Bake 30 minutes.

Pineapple Smoothie
(Serves 1)

A chilled, fruit-sweetened drink is a winning choice for a quick dose of flavor and nutrition. It's like an eggnog without the egg. Vary the fruit juice for an occasional change.

1 cup cold milk
1/2 banana, sliced
1 teaspoon sugar
1 teaspoon vanilla
2 tablespoons frozen concentrated pineapple or other
        fruit juice
Nutmeg

Place all ingredients except nutmeg in blender or food processor and blend until smooth. Pour into glass and sprinkle with nutmeg.

Chewing solutions
Prepare soups, stews or casserole dishes, all easy to chew, instead of chops and steaks.

Peachy Banana Shake
(Serves 1)

1/2 cup chopped fresh peach (or 1 jar chopped or
puréed baby food peaches)
1/2 cup milk, whole or skim
1/2 banana
2 tablespoons lemon juice
1/2 teaspoon minced lemon rind
Dash cloves

Mix all ingredients in blender or food processor until smooth.
Serve as drink or freeze as dessert.

Frozen Banana
(Serves 1)

A treat any time of day. Freezing creates a special texture and
brings out the natural sweetness of the fruit.

1 ripe banana
Plastic wrap

Peel banana and cut in fourths. Wrap in plastic and place in freezer.
Thaw banana slightly before eating.

Chewing Solutions
Have your teeth and gums checked regularly by your dentist.
If you have dentures, they may need to be replaced. Our gums
and facial muscles change as we age, and dentures may not fit
as well.

Breads

Super-Muffins
Bed-and-Breakfast Bran Muffins
Grandpa Hal's Waffles
Oatcakes
Wheat Sticks
Cornmeal Biscuits
Pineapple Danish
Granny's Baking Powder Biscuits
Hazel's Quick Coffee Cake
Best-Yet Walnut Bread
Orange-Honey Loaf
Blueberry Sweet Bread
Blueberry Oatmeal Muffins
Spicy Baked Pancake

Super-Muffins
(12-15 muffins)

One bowl, one fork and muffin tins — that's all you need to make these easy, light but filling treats. They pack a lot of nutrition and fiber into a small space, and they freeze well.

1 egg
1 cup milk
1/3 cup vegetable oil
1 cup white flour
1/2 cup whole wheat flour or whole wheat pastry flour
1/2 cup wheat germ
2 tablespoons bran (wheat or oat)
1 tablespoon baking powder
1/2 teaspoon salt
1/4 cup brown sugar
1/4 cup molasses
1/2 cup raisins
1/2 cup grated or finely chopped apple

Preheat oven to 375°. Mix egg, milk and oil in bowl. With a fork, stir in all other ingredients. Mixture will be lumpy. Spoon batter into muffin tins, greased or lined with cupcake papers. Fill 2/3 full. Bake 20 minutes.

Bake Small
Keep a supply of small containers, saucepans and baking pans on hand to make it easy to cook for one or two. Many dishes can be baked in custard cups, for example, which will also cut the baking time.

Bed-and-Breakfast Bran Muffins
(Makes 28-30 muffins)

ElRose Groves and her retired minister husband, Everett, served delightful breakfasts at their B&B cottage in Washington. ElRose's bran muffins are easy because you can mix up the batter at any time, and it keeps for two weeks in the refrigerator. You can bake and enjoy fresh muffins every morning.

> 1 cup boiling water
> 2 1/2 teaspoons baking soda
> 1/2 cup vegetable oil
> 1 cup sugar
> 2 eggs, beaten
> 2 cups buttermilk
> 1 1/2 cups flour
> 1 teaspoon salt
> 2 cups all-bran cereal
> 1 cup bran flake cereal
> 1 cup chopped dates or raisins
> 1 cup chopped nuts (optional)

Add soda to boiling water and allow to cool. Mix oil and sugar. Add eggs and stir in buttermilk. Add flour and salt alternately with water and soda mixture. Stir in cereals and dates or raisins. Cover batter and store in airtight container in refrigerator. May be stored up to 2 weeks. When ready to bake, preheat oven to 375°. Add nuts (if using them). Spoon batter into greased muffin tins. Bake 20 minutes or until muffins are light brown and toothpick inserted in center comes out clean.

Grandpa Hal's Waffles
(Makes approximately 4 waffles)

Hal Milton, a California minister and advisor and the author of *Wising Up: A Life Without Regrets*, likes to prepare these waffles for his grandchildren. He advises experimenting and being creative with additions — try using different grains, nuts, or dried fruits.

3/4 cup flour
1 teaspoon baking powder
1/2 cup old-fashioned oats
1 tablespoon oat bran
1/4 teaspoon salt
3/4 cup milk or water
2 tablespoons vegetable oil
1 egg, lightly beaten
2 tablespoons sunflower seeds

Preheat waffle iron; grease or spray with oil if necessary. Mix flour, baking powder, oats and salt. Add milk or water slowly. Add oil and mix. Add beaten egg and mix. Add sunflower seeds. Pour spoonfuls of batter into waffle iron and spread thinly. Cook until golden brown and crisp. Serve with maple or raspberry syrup.

Vitamin and Mineral Supplements: Do you need them?
The best source of advice on dietary supplements is your doctor or dietitian. Your balanced diet may be enough, or your individual needs may call for additional vitamins or minerals. Don't waste your money on unnecessary supplements, and don't endanger your health with megadoses. Get professional advice.

Oatcakes
(6 pancakes)

A hearty, nutty version of the usual breakfast pancake, this one is full of nutritious oats.

    1/2 cup flour
    1/3 cup uncooked oats
    1 tablespoon oat bran (optional)
    2 teaspoons baking powder
    1/4 teaspoon cinnamon
    1/2 cup low-fat or skim milk
    1 egg, beaten
    1 tablespoon vegetable oil or melted butter

Heat griddle or skillet and oil lightly. Combine all ingredients, stirring just until mixed. Spoon batter on hot griddle to size of cake desired. Turn once, when edges are lightly browned. Serve with jam, syrup or puréed fruit topping.

Wheat Sticks

Chewy and satisfying: a good substitute for bread or crackers.

    1 tablespoon honey
    1/4 cup vegetable oil
    1/2 cup milk
    1 cup whole wheat flour
    1 cup wheat germ
    1/2 teaspoon salt

Preheat oven to 325°. Blend honey, oil and milk. Add other ingredients and mix. Knead lightly on floured board. Roll dough into strips, 1 inch wide and 3 inches long. Place on ungreased baking sheet and bake 25 minutes. (For crisper sticks, roll thin and bake 20 minutes.)

Cornmeal Biscuits
(makes 6 3-inch biscuits - plus that small extra piece)

Piping hot from the oven, Esther MacLaren's cornmeal biscuits go well with almost any meal. For a touch of the South, serve them with ham and honey. Adding cheese ups the flavor quotient.

1 1/4 cups flour
3/4 cup cornmeal
4 teaspoons baking powder
1/2 teaspoon salt
1 tablespoon sugar
2 tablespoons shortening
2 tablespoons butter or margarine
3/4 cup milk
1/4 cup grated cheddar cheese (optional)

Preheat oven to 450°. Sift dry ingredients. Blend in shortening and butter or margarine with a pastry blender, or cut in using two knives. Add milk, stirring lightly with fork. Add cheese (if using it). Knead dough lightly. Roll to 1/2 inch thickness and cut with 2-inch or 3-inch cookie cutter. Place on ungreased baking sheet and bake 15 minutes.

Pineapple Danish
(Serves 1)

1 slice whole wheat toast
1 tablespoon cream cheese or small-curd cottage cheese
1 slice canned pineapple or 2 tablespoons
       crushed pineapple
1/4 teaspoon cinnamon
Dash nutmeg

Preheat broiler. Spread toast with cheese. Top with pineapple and sprinkle with spices. Broil until heated, about 3 minutes.

Granny's Baking Powder Biscuits

Your grandchildren will have fun cutting these biscuits into different shapes with cookie cutters.

    1 cup flour
    2 tablespoons wheat germ
    1 tablespoon baking powder
    1/2 teaspoon salt
    2 tablespoons vegetable oil
    5 tablespoons milk

Preheat oven to 400°. Combine dry ingredients. Mix oil and milk and stir into flour mixture. Place dough between two sheets of waxed paper and knead lightly. Roll out 1/2-inch thick and cut with biscuit cutter. Place on baking sheet and bake 12 minutes, until browned.

Hazel's Quick Coffee Cake

Hazel Jensen first tried this recipe fifty years ago. It's been a breakfast standby for her family and an afternoon treat for many visitors ever since.

    2 cups flour
    2 teaspoons baking powder
    1/2 teaspoon salt
    1/2 cup sugar
    1/4 teaspoon mace
    1 egg, beaten
    1 cup milk
    2 tablespoons melted butter

Preheat oven to 425°. Mix dry ingredients. Add egg, milk and butter and mix. Pour into buttered 8-inch baking pan and sprinkle with topping. Bake 20 minutes.

Topping
>   2 tablespoons flour
>   1/2 teaspoon cinnamon
>   2 tablespoons brown sugar
>   1 tablespoon soft butter

Mix all ingredients until crumbly.

Best-Yet Walnut Bread
(One 8x4-inch loaf pan)

Beth Donaldson perfected this recipe for a bread festive enough for teatime but hearty enough for lunch sandwiches. It's lower in fat than many sweet breads because it contains no butter or oil.

>   1 egg
>   1 cup sugar
>   3 cups sifted flour
>   2 tablespoons wheat germ
>   1 teaspoon salt
>   4 teaspoons baking powder
>   1 cup milk
>   1 cup coarsely chopped walnuts

Preheat oven to 350°. Combine egg and sugar and beat well. Mix in all other ingredients except nuts. Stir in nuts. Spoon into greased loaf pan and bake 1 hour or until toothpick inserted in center comes out clean.

Orange-Honey Loaf
(One 5x9-inch loaf pan)

An orange-flavored, cake-like bread that keeps well. Soaked with a marmalade glaze, it's delicious for breakfast, afternoon tea, or dessert at dinner.

> 1/2 cup butter or margarine
> 1/2 cup honey
> 2 eggs, beaten
> 3 tablespoons orange marmalade
> 1 1/2 cups flour
> 2 tablespoons baking powder
> 1/4 teaspoon salt
> 1/4 teaspoon baking soda
> 1 tablespoon grated orange or lemon peel
> 1/3 cup chopped nuts

Preheat oven to 325°. Mix butter and honey. Add eggs and marmalade and beat well. Add flour, baking powder, salt and soda, and mix. Stir in orange or lemon peel and nuts. Pour into buttered loaf pan. Bake 50 minutes. Pierce top with fork at 1-inch intervals and pour glaze over.

Glaze
> 1 tablespoon butter or margarine
> 2 tablespoons orange marmalade
> 2 tablespoons powdered confectioner's sugar

Melt butter in saucepan. Stir in marmalade and heat. Add sugar, stir and heat.

Blueberry Sweet Bread
One 9x5-inch loaf pan

Bursting with juicy blueberries, this is a tea bread that doubles as a dessert cake, topped with whipped cream, ice cream or frozen yogurt. It was contributed by Esther MacLaren, who cautioned that it's best to use frozen, unthawed berries.

    2 cups flour
    1/2 cup sugar
    2 teaspoons baking powder
    1/2 teaspoon salt
    1/2 teaspoon baking soda
    2 teaspoons grated orange peel
    2 cups frozen blueberries
    1 egg, lightly beaten
    3/4 cup orange juice
    2 tablespoons vegetable oil

Topping
    3 tablespoons sugar
    1 tablespoon cinnamon
    2 tablespoons melted butter or margarine

Preheat oven to 350°. With fork or wooden spoon, mix flour, sugar, salt, soda, baking powder and orange peel. Fold in blueberries. Add egg, orange juice and oil, stirring carefully. Spoon batter into greased 9x5-inch loaf pan (batter will be thick). Mix topping ingredients and sprinkle on bread batter. Bake 60 minutes or until toothpick inserted in center comes out clean.

Blueberry Oatmeal Muffins
(Makes about 12)

Esther MacLaren, always noted for her efficiency, kept the dry ingredients for this recipe in a quart jar in the cupboard. When she was ready to bake, all she had to do was add the liquids. The result is a flavorful, nutritious muffin that is good any time of day.

- 1 1/4 cups oats
- 1 cup whole wheat flour
- 1 tablespoon baking powder
- 1/3 cup sugar
- 1/2 teaspoon salt
- 1 cup milk
- 1 egg, lightly beaten
- 1/4 cup vegetable oil
- 3/4 cup blueberries, fresh or frozen

Preheat oven to 425°. Combine dry ingredients. Add egg, milk and oil and stir just until blended. Stir in berries. Spoon into greased muffin tins or tins lined with cupcake papers. Bake 20-25 minutes.

Avoid Spoilage

As our senses dim with age, we run a greater risk of eating foods that have lost their freshness. Watch the dates on milk and yogurt cartons, and don't keep opened foods longer than a few days in the refrigerator. Fresh meat should not be kept longer than one or, at the most, two days before cooking. If in doubt, throw it out. Saving a few cents is not worth the risk to your health.

Spicy Baked Pancake
(Serves 1)

This light pancake puffs to a golden brown as it bakes. Philip Shaw, who contributed the recipe, doubles it to serve two generously when he's making a weekend brunch. Served with an assortment of jams, hot coffee, and a dish of fresh fruit on the side, it makes a toothsome meal that is easy to prepare.

    1 egg, lightly beaten
    1/4 cup flour
    1/4 cup milk
    1/8 teaspoon Mixed Sweet Spices
    1 tablespoon butter or margarine
    1 tablespoon confectioner's powdered sugar
    Lemon wedge

Preheat oven to 400°. Combine egg, milk, flour and spices and mix to form lumpy batter. Melt butter or margarine in oven-proof skillet. Pour in batter. Bake 15 minutes, until pancake is golden brown. Sprinkle with sugar and lemon juice.

Desserts

Blueberry Flummery
Apple-Cran Crisp
Charles Jordan's Famous Banana Pudding
Betty's Lemon Cake Pudding
Pineapple Betty
Pink Poached Pears
Fruit Sorbet
Spicy Peach Cobbler
Dessert Topping
Date-Nut Squares
Rich & Easy Chocolate Pudding
Aunt Esther's Wacky Cake
Apple Spice Cake
Sweet Potato Pudding
Holiday's Apple Cake
Oat Wheat Cookies
Frozen Fruity Yogurt
Yogurt Banana Split
Vyra's Prune Cake
Peach-Lemon Crisp
Fruit With Yogurt-Ginger Sauce
Bernice's Oatmeal Cookies
Coconut Squares
Peanut Butter Squares
Prune-Apple Bars
Vera's Strawberry Pie
Grandma Parkhurst's Blueberry Pie
Chocolate Applesauce Cake
Star Cookies
Cherry Crumb Crunch
Edith's Oatmeal Cookies
Chocolate-Peanut Butter Balls
Candied Mint and Roses
Low Cholesterol Banana-Pineapple Cookies

Blueberry Flummery
(Serves 2)

1 tablespoon cornstarch
1/4 cup sugar
3/4 cup water
1 cup blueberries, fresh or frozen
Juice and grated rind of 1 lemon
1/4 teaspoon Mixed Sweet Spices

Mix cornstarch and sugar in saucepan. Add all other ingredients. Cook over medium heat, stirring, until slightly thickened. Chill and serve alone or as a sauce on coffee cake, Vyra's Prune Cake (page 153) or Orange-Honey Loaf (page 136).

Apple-Cran Crisp
(Serves 3)

2 cooking apples, peeled and sliced
1 tablespoon lemon juice
1/4 cup apple juice
3 tablespoons cranberry sauce, fresh or canned
3 tablespoons flour
3 tablespoons oats
3 tablespoons brown sugar
3 tablespoons butter or margarine, softened
1 teaspoon Mixed Sweet Spices

Preheat oven to 350°. Place apples and cranberry sauce in buttered baking dish. Pour apple juice and lemon juice over. In a bowl, mix all other ingredients with fork or fingers and spoon over apple mixture. Cover and bake for 20 minutes. Remove cover and bake another 10 minutes. Serve warm, plain or with milk or cream.

Charles Jordan's Famous Banana Pudding
(Serves 4-6)

Charles Jordan, retired Director of Parks and Recreation and former city commissioner in Portland, Oregon, is too busy serving on the boards of numerous charitable and conservation organizations to spend much time cooking. When he does, this is the dish he's best known for, a dessert from his southern roots. For a richer taste, Charles uses evaporated milk, with less cornstarch.

> 2 egg yolks
> 3/4 cup sugar
> 1/4 cup cornstarch
> 2 cups milk
> 1 tablespoon banana extract or 1 teaspoon vanilla
> 2 bananas, sliced
> Vanilla wafers

Line a serving bowl with vanilla wafers. Cover wafers with banana slices. Beat egg yolks with a fork and set aside. Heat milk in saucepan until steaming; do not boil. Remove from heat and add vanilla or banana extract. Place cornstarch and sugar in bowl and stir well. Add milk, stirring. Add egg yolks gradually, stirring constantly. Pour mixture into saucepan or double boiler and heat, stirring constantly until slightly thickened. Pour over bananas and wafers (this can be done in alternating layers of bananas and milk mixture). Top with more vanilla wafers. Chill and serve.

Convenience Foods?
Some "instant" packaged foods offer a saving in time and effort and are well worth the expense. Others are not only expensive, they may be high in sodium, fat and preservatives. Protect yourself by using fresh foods where possible, with the occasional addition of a favorite package.

Betty's Lemon Cake Pudding

This tangy dessert has been a favorite with Betty Parkhurst's family in Illinois for 40 years.

1 egg, separated
1/3 cup sugar
3 tablespoons flour
Dash salt
1 teaspoon grated lemon rind
1/2 cup milk
2 1/2 tablespoons lemon juice

Preheat oven to 350°. Beat egg white until stiff peaks form. In another bowl, mix sugar, salt, flour and lemon rind. Add yolk and milk and mix well. Add lemon juice. Fold in egg whites. Mixture will be lumpy. Pour into buttered baking dish. Set in pan of hot water and bake 35-40 minutes.

Pineapple Betty
(Serves 2)

Bread pudding texture, with a dash of fruity, spicy pineapple. Delicious when served warm with milk or ice cream.

1 slice stale bread
1/2 cup crushed pineapple
1 tablespoon brown sugar
2 teaspoons butter or margarine
1/2 teaspoon Mixed Sweet Spices

Preheat oven to 350°. Cut bread into cubes and sprinkle in buttered baking dish. Cover with pineapple and sugar. Dot with butter and sprinkle with spices. Bake 30 minutes.

Pink Poached Pears
(Serves 2)

Try this simple but pretty dessert with a sprinkling of fresh raspberries.

> 1 ripe pear
> 1 cup cranberry juice or 3 tablespoons raspberry-cranberry
>   frozen concentrate with enough water to make
>   1 cup liquid
> Pinch of cinnamon
> 1 teaspoon lemon juice
> 1/2 teaspoon lemon rind, shredded

Peel the pear, slice in half lengthwise, and remove core. Place pear and all other ingredients in saucepan. Bring liquid to a boil, cover, and simmer for 10 minutes. Turn pears and simmer 5 more minutes, until tender. (Length of time depends upon type of pear). Serve warm or chilled, with a spoonful of the liquid.

Fruit Sorbet

Here's a sherbet substitute with fresh fruit flavor and icy texture. Nectarines, peaches and berries work well.

> 1 cup fresh or packaged frozen fruit
> 2 tablespoons water or fruit juice
> 1 tablespoon sugar
> 1 tablespoon lemon juice

If using fresh fruit, chop and place in bowl in freezer. When partially frozen, remove. If using packaged fruit, partially thaw. Dissolve sugar in water or fruit juice. Stir dissolved sugar and lemon juice into fruit. Refreeze.

Spicy Peach Cobbler
(Serves 2)

1 cup chopped or sliced peaches, fresh, frozen or
    canned and drained
1/4 cup sugar
1/2 teaspoon Mixed Sweet Spices
1 tablespoon water
1/2 cup flour
1/2 teaspoon baking powder
1 tablespoon sugar
2 tablespoons butter
1/3 cup milk

Preheat oven to 400°. In saucepan, mix peaches, sugar, spices
and water. Heat and stir. In bowl, mix flour, baking powder and
sugar. Cut in butter with pastry blender or fingers to make a coarse
mixture. Stir in milk. Place hot peach mixture in baking dish.
Spoon flour mixture over peaches. Bake 20 minutes, until top is
golden brown.

Dessert Topping
(Serves 2)

2 tablespoons ice water
2 tablespoons instant non-fat powdered milk
2 tablespoons sugar
2 tablespoons lemon juice

Slowly add powdered milk to ice water, beating until stiff peaks
form (5 to 8 minutes). Add sugar and lemon juice. Chill.

Date-Nut Squares
(One 8-inch-square pan)

Esther McLeod contributed this sweet and chewy, easy-to-make treat.

> 2 egg whites (large eggs)
> 1/4 cup sugar
> 1/2 teaspoon baking powder
> 7 saltines (soda crackers), rolled to make fine crumbs
> 1/4 cup chopped dates
> 1/4 cup chopped nuts

Preheat oven to 300°. Beat egg whites until foamy. Slowly add sugar and baking powder, continuing to beat until soft peaks form. Fold in cracker crumbs, dates and nuts. Spoon into buttered baking pan. Bake 40 minutes. Cut into squares.

Rich & Easy Chocolate Pudding
(Serves 2)

Any chocolate-loving grandchild will come back for seconds on this creamy good dessert.

> 3 tablespoons baking cocoa
> 1/3 cup sugar
> 1 tablespoon cornstarch
> 1 cup milk
> 1 egg yolk
> 1/2 teaspoon vanilla

In saucepan, mix cocoa, sugar, and cornstarch. Add milk and mix well with whisk. Over medium heat, gradually add egg yolk. Stir constantly with whisk until smooth and thickened. Remove from heat and stir in vanilla. Chill.

Aunt Esther's Wacky Cake
(One 8-inch square pan)

A chocolatey-good dessert in great demand for 3 generations of Esther MacLaren's family reunions. Esther always said, "When I first tried this recipe, I didn't believe it would work. But it does!"

1 1/2 cups flour
1 cup sugar
1 teaspoon baking soda
3 tablespoons baking cocoa
1 teaspoon salt
1 teaspoon vanilla
5 tablespoons vegetable oil
1 tablespoon vinegar
1 cup cold water
1/2 cup chopped nuts (optional)

Preheat oven to 325°. Sift flour, sugar, baking soda, cocoa and salt directly into 8-inch square baking pan. Make 3 hollows in mixture. In one hollow, pour vanilla. In another, pour vinegar. In the third, pour oil. Pour water over all and stir until smooth. If nuts are used, sprinkle over batter. Bake 30-35 minutes or until toothpick inserted in center comes out clean.

Vitamin D
A well-balanced diet and regular outdoor activity give some of us the Vitamin D we require, but a supplement may be needed for bone strength. Consult your doctor or dietitian before taking extra Vitamin D.

Apple Spice Cake
(One 8-inch-square pan)

1/4 cup flour
1 1/2 teaspoons baking soda
1/2 teaspoon salt
1 teaspoon Mixed Sweet Spices
1 tablespoon baking cocoa
1/2 cup sugar
1/3 cup vegetable oil
1 cup unsweetened applesauce
1/4 cup raisins
1/4 cup chopped nuts (optional)

Preheat oven to 375°. Mix flour, soda, salt, sugar, spices and cocoa. In another bowl, combine oil and applesauce. Add flour mixture and beat until smooth. Stir in nuts and raisins. Pour batter into greased baking pan. Bake 45 minutes. Serve topped with applesauce.

Sweet Potato Pudding
(Serves 2 generously)
Rich flavor in a not-too-sweet dessert.

1 egg
3/4 cup evaporated milk
3/4 cup cooked, mashed sweet potatoes or yams
1/4 cup brown sugar
Dash salt
1 teaspoon Mixed Sweet Spices

Preheat oven to 350°. Place all ingredients in blender and mix until smooth. Pour mixture into baking dish. Bake 35-40 minutes.

Holiday's Apple Cake

Holiday Johnson, a noted yoga teacher based in Portland, Oregon, says her daughters know this recipe by heart, and the grandchildren love it. It's known as the "whatever's on hand" dessert because almost any flour works, and any addition you care to mix in.

> 4 cups apples, unpeeled and coarsely chopped (cut
>   quarters in fourths)
> 1/3 cup vegetable oil
> 1/2 cup sugar
> 1 cup flour (any type, but not entirely whole wheat)
> 1 egg (or egg substitute), beaten
> 1 teaspoon good-quality cinnamon
> 1/4 teaspoon nutmeg
> 1/8 teaspoon salt
> 1/2 teaspoon baking soda
> 1/2 teaspoon vanilla
> 1/4 cup chopped nuts, dates or raisins

Preheat oven to 350°. Mix oil with apple pieces in a large bowl. Stir in sugar. Stir in beaten egg or substitute. Add spices, nuts and raisins or other additions. Add vanilla. Sprinkle flour over mixture. Sprinkle soda over mixture. Stir well. Batter will be thick. Spoon into 8" or 9"-square baking pan. Bake 45 minutes or until apples are soft and toothpick inserted in center comes out clean.

On A Budget
If you're a shopper on a budget (and who isn't?), choose wisely. Buy sale items in quantity and divide your purchases into smaller packages for the freezer (be sure to label them clearly). Try splitting costs and purchases with a friend or relative.

Oat Wheat Cookies

1/2 cup shortening
1/4 cup butter or margarine
1/4 cup white sugar
3/4 cup brown sugar
2 eggs
1 teaspoon vanilla
1 teaspoon lemon rind, grated or minced
2 tablespoons molasses
1 1/2 cups flour
2 tablespoons wheat germ
2 tablespoons oat bran
2 cups oats
1 teaspoon baking soda
1/2 teaspoon salt
1/2 teaspoon Mixed Sweet Spices
1 cup raisins, coconut, nuts or dates if desired

Preheat oven to 375°. Mix shortening, butter and sugar and beat until creamy. Add eggs, vanilla and lemon rind. Add all other ingredients and mix well. Place walnut-sized pieces of dough on baking sheet. Bake 12 minutes.

Frozen Fruity Yogurt
(1 serving)

1/2 cup plain yogurt
1/2 cup chopped fresh or canned, drained fruit
1/4 teaspoon vanilla
1 teaspoon sugar or honey.

Mix all ingredients and freeze until slushy. Stir and refreeze. Allow to thaw slightly before serving.

Yogurt Banana Split
(Serves 1)

1/2 cup plain yogurt
3 tablespoons fresh or frozen strawberries
1/2 banana
Chopped nuts
Honey or heated strawberry jam
Dessert Topping (optional — see page 147)
Chopped nuts

Spoon yogurt into dessert bowl. Spoon strawberries over yogurt. Slice bananas lengthwise and place on either side of yogurt. Drizzle honey or jam over all. Top with whipped topping and nuts.

Vyra's Prune Cake
(One 8-inch-square pan)

This fruit-filled goodie is especially good with a dollop of applesauce on top.

1/2 cup sugar
2 tablespoons butter or margarine
2 eggs
1/2 cup cooked, chopped prunes
1 teaspoon baking soda dissolved in 1 tablespoon
       prune juice
1 cup white or whole wheat flour
1 teaspoon Mixed Sweet Spices
1 teaspoon baking powder

Preheat oven to 350°. Beat sugar, butter and eggs until creamy. Add prunes and juice with dissolved baking soda. Add flour, spices and baking powder and mix well. Spoon into greased 8-inch-square pan. Bake 25-30 minutes.

Peach-Lemon Crisp
(Serves 2)

2 cups peaches, peeled and chopped or sliced
4 tablespoons apple juice
1 tablespoon lemon juice
1 teaspoon cornstarch
3 tablespoons brown sugar
1 teaspoon lemon zest
2 tablespoons flour
1/4 teaspoon nutmeg
1/4 cup oats
1 tablespoon chopped nuts (optional)

Preheat oven to 350°. In saucepan, mix peaches, 2 tablespoons of apple juice, lemon juice, cornstarch, 2 tablespoons of brown sugar, and lemon zest. Simmer and stir until thickened. In bowl, mix 1 tablespoon brown sugar, 2 tablespoons apple juice, flour, nutmeg, oats, oat bran and nuts if using. Place hot fruit in baking dish. Top fruit with spoonfuls of flour mixture. Bake 20 minutes, until crisp and golden brown.

Fruit With Yogurt-Ginger Sauce
(Serves 1)

Tropical fruits and creamy-smooth yogurt, with a touch of ginger, create a delicious, light dessert.

1/4 cup pineapple chunks
2 tablespoons flaked coconut
1/2 banana, chopped
1 teaspoon chopped fresh ginger
2 tablespoons plain, low-fat yogurt
1 teaspoon honey
1 teaspoon orange or pineapple juice

Mix all ingredients, chill and serve.

Bernice's Oatmeal Cookies
(About 75 small cookies)

Bernice Peck, well aware of the value of oats to good health, often baked these flavorful cookies.

- 1/2 cup shortening
- 1/2 cup butter
- 3/4 cup sugar
- 2 eggs
- 2 cups oats
- 1 cup flour
- 1/2 teaspoon baking soda
- 1/3 cup milk
- 1 teaspoon cinnamon
- 1 teaspoon vanilla
- 1/2 teaspoon salt
- 1/2 cup raisins, chopped nuts, or chopped dates (optional)

Preheat oven to 350°. Beat shortening, sugar and eggs until creamy. Mix in all other ingredients except nuts, raisins or dates. Stir in nuts, raisins or dates. Place spoonfuls of dough on baking sheet. Bake 8-10 minutes.

Supermarket Service
Most supermarkets and grocery stores will help with extra service, if you request it. If you want just half a squash or cabbage; if you prefer only 1 lamb chop or ½ pound of ground beef; if you'd like 6 eggs instead of a dozen — ask. The clerk or butcher is there to serve you.

Coconut Squares
(One 8-inch-square pan)

1 1/4 cups flour
1/2 cup (1 stick) butter or margarine
2 teaspoons brown sugar

Preheat oven to 350°. Mix ingredients and press into baking pan. Pour filling over.

Filling

1/2 cup brown sugar
2 eggs, lightly beaten
1 cup flaked coconut
1/2 cup chopped walnuts
1 teaspoon vanilla

Mix all ingredients and pour over first mixture in baking pan. Bake 35 minutes.

Peanut Butter Squares
(One 8-inch-square pan)

A chewy dessert with peanut protein, perfected by Hilda Janowski, a peanut butter lover into her retirement years. The grandchildren will love these cookies and they probably won't object if you drizzle chocolate sauce over them.

1/3 cup peanut butter, creamy or chunky style
1/3 cup butter or margarine
1/2 teaspoon vanilla
3/4 cup brown sugar
1/4 teaspoon salt
1 egg (or 1/4 cup frozen egg substitute)
2/3 cup flour
1 tablespoon wheat germ
1/4 cup chopped peanuts (optional)

Preheat oven to 350°. Mix peanut butter and butter. Add vanilla, sugar, salt and egg and blend well. Add flour and wheat germ and beat until smooth. Stir in nuts. Sprinkle with more chopped nuts if desired and spread in buttered baking pan. Bake 30 minutes. Cut into squares.

Prune-Apple Bars
(One 8-inch-square baking pan)

Natural sweetness sandwiched between nutritious grains.

> 1/2 cup brown sugar
> 2/3 cup flour
> 1/2 teaspoon salt
> 1/4 teaspoon baking soda
> 1 cup rolled oats, regular or quick-cooking
> 2 tablespoons oat bran
> 1 teaspoon lemon or orange zest
> 1 1/2 teaspoons Mixed Sweet Spices
> 6 tablespoons butter or margarine, melted
> 1 cup applesauce
> 1/2 cup cooked chopped prunes

Preheat oven to 375°. Combine all dry ingredients and orange or lemon zest. Add melted butter and mix. Spoon half of mixture into greased 8-inch baking pan and press with hand or spatula. Mix applesauce and chopped prunes and spread over flour mixture. Top with remaining flour mixture. Bake 20 minutes, until golden brown.

Vera's Strawberry Pie

Vera Porter shared her favorite strawberry pie recipe, saying that it couldn't be easier. She uses a purchased pie shell and packaged pudding.

> 1 baked pie shell
> 2 cups fresh strawberries, hulled and sliced
>   (save a few for garnish)
> 2 cups vanilla pudding, homemade or packaged
> Whipped dessert topping, purchased or homemade (p 147)

Stir berries into prepared, cooled pudding. Spoon into pie shell and top with whipped topping. Garnish with a few strawberries. Chill.

Grandma Parkhurst's Blueberry Pie
(Makes one 8- or 9-inch pie)

Kathy Fagan contributes her Grandma Parkhurst's foolproof recipe for blueberry pie. She remembers savoring the pie many times with her grandmother, an excellent cook.

> Pie crust for shell and top
> 2 cups blueberries, fresh or frozen
> 2/3 cup sugar
> 2 teaspoons lemon juice
> 1 1/2 tablespoons flour
> 1 tablespoon butter

Preheat oven to 400°. In a bowl, mix berries, sugar, lemon juice and flour. Pour into pie shell in pie pan. Dot filling with bits of butter. Cover with top crust. With a sharp knife, make several slashes in crust. Sprinkle with sugar. Bake 30 minutes, until crust is golden brown.

Chocolate Applesauce Cake
(One 8-inch baking pan)

Edith Owenbey said this recipe came from a pioneer family in Utah. Moist and spicy, the cake is as popular as ever. It keeps well, refrigerated.

    1/2 cup sugar
    1 cup flour
    1/2 teaspoon cinnamon
    1/2 teaspoon nutmeg
    1/2 teaspoon cloves
    1 1/2 teaspoons cornstarch
    2 tablespoons unsweetened cocoa
    1/2 cup melted butter or vegetable oil
    3/4 cup unsweetened applesauce
    1 teaspoon baking soda
    1 cup nuts, raisins or candied fruit if desired

Preheat oven to 350°. Mix sugar, flour, spices, cornstarch and cocoa. Stir in butter and oil. In separate bowl add baking soda to applesauce. Mix with batter. Add nuts and raisins if desired. Pour into 8-inch baking pan. Bake 50-60 minutes, until toothpick inserted in center comes out clean.

Food Storage
Use your refrigerator to store items often kept in the cupboard. Raisins, nuts, bread, coffee, jams, jellies and peanut butter will all keep longer if chilled.

Star Cookies

Another of Vera Porter's specialties, these rich cookies are easy to make and festive for holidays. Grandchildren like to press the chocolates into the cookies.

> 1 cup good-quality butter
> 2 cups flour
> 1/2 cup sugar
> 1/2 cup finely chopped nuts
> Chocolate candy "stars" (not easily available nowadays,
>   but a Hershey's Kiss works just as well)

Mix all ingredients except chocolate. Chill dough several hours or overnight. Preheat oven to 350°. Shape dough into walnut-sized balls and place on baking sheet. Bake 10 minutes. Remove from oven and press a chocolate star or kiss into each cookie. Return to oven for 5 minutes.

Cherry Crumb Crunch
(One 8-inch-square pan)

Esther MacLaren's afternoon and after-dinner visitors gave this unusual dessert a top rating. It gets compliments every time it is served.

> 1/4 cup butter or margarine
> 3/4 cup flour
> 1/2 cup brown sugar
> 1/2 cup oats
> 1/2 cup chopped nuts (optional)
> 1/4 teaspoon baking soda
> 1/4 teaspoon salt
> 1/4 teaspoon cloves
> 1 can (16-ounce) pitted pie cherries, drained

Preheat oven to 350°. Combine all ingredients except cherries. Mix with fingers until crumbly. Spread half of mixture in 8-inch baking pan. Spoon cherries over. Top with remaining crumb mixture. Bake 30-35 minutes.

Edith's Oatmeal Cookies
(About 32 cookies)

Another of Edith Owenbey's contributions, these delectable morsels will add oats to your diet.

> 1/2 cup white sugar
> 1/2 cup brown sugar
> 1/2 cup shortening
> 1 egg
> 1 cup oats
> 1 cup flour
> 1/2 teaspoon baking soda dissolved in 1 teaspoon
>   hot water
> 1/2 teaspoon salt
> 1/2 teaspoon vanilla
> 1/2 cup chopped nuts or raisins if desired

Preheat oven to 350°. Beat sugar, shortening and egg until smooth. Add all other ingredients and mix. Place by spoonfuls on baking sheet and bake 12-15 minutes.

Chocolate-Peanut Butter Balls

For that once-in-a-while taste of fudgy-rich candy, try these easy, no-bake chocolate balls. Grandchildren can help to make them.

        2 tablespoons butter
        1/4 cup sugar
        1 package (1/2 cup) instant oatmeal, cinnamon-spice
                flavor preferred, or 1/2 cup quick-cooking oats
        2 tablespoons peanut butter, creamy or crunchy style
        1 tablespoon baking cocoa
        1/4 teaspoon vanilla
        1 tablespoon water (more if needed for mixture to
                hold together)
        Finely chopped coconut shreds, candy sprinkles,
                and/or finely chopped peanuts

In a bowl, mix all ingredients except coconut, sprinkles and nuts. Form into 1-inch balls (moistened hands help with soft dough). Roll balls in coconut, sprinkles, and/or nuts. Place on plate in single layer and refrigerate to chill.

Candied Mint and Roses

Making these sweet, mint-flavored treats is fun for grandparents and children alike. The result is both crunchy and chewy. The pretty leaves and petals add a decorative touch to desserts.

        1/3 cup fresh mint leaves and flower petals (roses,
                day lilies, gladiolas, and violets are good choices)
        1 egg white, lightly beaten
        1/3 cup sugar
        3-4 drops peppermint extract

Preheat oven to 225°. Wash and dry leaves and petals. Use only leaves and flowers that have NOT been treated with chemicals. Add peppermint extract to sugar and stir well (back of spoon helps smooth lumps). Dip leaves and petals in beaten egg white to coat, then in flavored sugar. Place on baking sheet or aluminum foil. Bake for 20 minutes, until dry and crisp.

Low Cholesterol Banana-Pineapple Cookies

Even when you are avoiding foods with cholesterol, you can have a touch of sweetness with these cake-like puffs. The flavor and texture is similar to banana bread.

> 1 egg white
> 1/4 cup mashed ripe banana (1/2 medium banana)
> 1/4 cup crushed water-packed pineapple with juice
> 1/4 cup polyunsaturated vegetable oil
> 1 tablespoon skim milk
> 1 cup flour
> 1 tablespoon brown sugar
> 1/4 teaspoon baking soda
> 1/4 teaspoon salt
> 1/4 teaspoon cloves
> 1/4 cup flaked coconut

Preheat oven to 350°. Mix egg white, banana, pineapple, oil and milk. Beat in all other ingredients. Place by spoonfuls on baking sheet. Bake 8-10 minutes, until golden brown. Do not overbake; the cookies should be light in color.

Menus

In these day-by-day breakfast and dinner menus, dishes with recipes in this book are marked in bold print, and the page number of the recipe is indicated in parentheses.

You may wish to follow the menus in the order given, or pick and choose from the recipes you prefer.

Coffee, tea and milk have not been included in the menus, but they may be added to each meal. Be sure to serve water with every meal, as well.

Week 1

Sunday Breakfast
Light Menu
Orange Juice with squeeze of Lemon
Whole Wheat Toast with Peanut Butter and sprinkle of Cinnamon
Hearty Menu
Orange Juice with squeeze of Lemon
Eggs Benedict (page 87)

Sunday Dinner
Light Menu
Tomato Juice with Dash of Hot Pepper Sauce
Tuna au Gratin (page 75)
Minty Fruit Salad (page 124)
Bernice's Oatmeal Cookies (page 155)
Hearty Menu
One-Pot Pot Roast (page 17)
Minty Fruit Salad (page 124)
Bernice's Oatmeal Cookies (page 155)

Monday Breakfast
Light Menu
1/2 Grapefruit, cut into chunks
Instant Hot Cereal with Milk and Honey or Brown Sugar
Hearty Menu
1/2 Grapefruit, cut into chunks
French Toast with Butter or Margarine and Syrup or Fruit Purée

Monday Dinner
Light Menu
Not-Quite Quiche (page 88)
Tossed Green Salad with Dressing
Applesauce
Hearty Menu
Meat and Potatoes (page 18)
Pineapple-Carrots (page 114)
Tossed Green Salad with Dressing
Applesauce and Cookies

Tuesday Breakfast
Light Menu
Tangerine Segments
Bran Muffin with Butter, Margarine, or Cream Cheese and Jam
Hearty Menu
Fruit Juice or Cut-Up Fruit
Cornmeal Biscuits (page 133) with Butter or Margarine and Honey
Scrambled Egg and Low-Fat Sausage Links

Tuesday Dinner
Light Menu
Mushroom-Zucchini Frittata (page 91)
Steamed Green Beans with Dill and Grated Cheese
French Bread with Butter or Margarine
Hearty Menu
Baked Chicken (page 48)
Baked Potato, topped with Yogurt and Chives
Green Beans Parmesan (page 113)
Flavored Gelatin with Fruit

Wednesday Breakfast
Light Menu
Plain, Low-Fat Yogurt with Chopped Fruit, sprinkled with Granola (or other fiber-rich cereal)
Slice of Orange-Honey Loaf (page 136)
Hearty Menu
Pineapple Juice
Oatmeal with Raisins
Slice of Orange-Honey Loaf (page 136)

Wednesday Dinner
Light Menu
Penny's Thousand-Year Chicken Soup (page 102)
French Bread, toasted
Tomato Slices with Chopped Lettuce and Parsley
Hearty Menu
Cranberry Pork Steaks (page 33)
Cooked Corn (canned, frozen or fresh)
Tomato and Cucumber Slices on Lettuce, with Chopped Parsley
French Bread, toasted
Betty's Lemon Cake Pudding (page 145)

Thursday Breakfast
Light Menu
Cottage Cheese with Crushed Pineapple and Dash of Nutmeg
Super-Muffins (page 129)
Hearty Menu
Grapefruit Juice
Scrambled Eggs with Grated Cheese and Chives
Super-Muffins (page 129)

Thursday Dinner
Light Menu
Cheese Soubise (page 84)
Waldorf Delight (page 117)
Tangerine or Orange segments

Hearty Menu
Dr. B's Cheese Enchiladas (page 82)
Salad of tossed leafy greens
Tangerine or Orange Slices

Friday Breakfast
Light Menu
Melon Wedge with Squeeze of Lemon
Oatmeal Cookie spread with Peanut Butter
Hearty Menu
Melon Wedge with squeeze of Lemon
Frozen, Toasted Waffles with Butter or Margarine and Syrup or Fruit Purée
Baked Ham Slice, heated

Friday Dinner
Light Menu
Garden Stew (page 105)
Cornmeal Biscuits (page 133) or Granny's Biscuits (page 134)
Prune-Apple Bars (page 157)
Hearty Menu
Fish with Lemon Sauce (page 63)
Rice, white or brown, with chopped Almonds and Parsley
Chopped Lettuce Salad with Tomato Wedges
Prune-Apple Bars (page 157)

Saturday Breakfast
Light Menu
Cereal Parfait (Cold Cereal, Chopped Fruit, and Ice Cream layered in a parfait glass)
Hearty Menu
Orange Juice
Egg-in-a-Nest (page 90)

Saturday Dinner
Light Menu
Creamy Tomato Soup (page 96)
Oyster Crackers
Mixed Green Salad: Lettuce, Spinach, and Green Pepper with Lemon Juice
Fruit Sorbet (page 146)
Hearty Menu
Prime-Time Pizza (page 26)
Finger-Food Salad (Carrot and Celery Sticks with Chunks of Broccoli and Green Bell Pepper)
Fruit Sorbet (page 146)
Cookie

Week 2

Sunday Breakfast
Light Menu
Fruit Juice
Poached Egg on Rye Toast
Hearty Menu
Stewed Prunes
Hot Cereal with Chopped Apples, Raisins and Cinnamon

Sunday Dinner
Light Menu
Ginger-Coconut Chicken (page 49)
Mixed Salad with Dressing: Lettuce, Cucumber, Parsley and Tomato
Frozen Fruity Yogurt (page 152)
Hearty Menu
Jambalaya Chicken (page 57)
Dinner Roll with Butter or Margarine
Chopped Lettuce Salad with Dressing
Peanut Butter Squares (page 156)

Monday Breakfast
Light Menu
Orange Slice with Flaked Coconut
Cold Cereal and Milk topped with Sliced Banana and dash of Allspice
Hearty Menu
Orange Slice with Flaked Coconut
Onion-Pepper Omelet (page 80)
Whole Wheat Toast with Butter or Margarine and Jam

Monday Dinner
Light Menu
Chicken-Stuffed Tomato (page 52)
Biscuit or Whole Wheat Toast with Butter or Margarine
Hearty Menu
Chicken Cobbler (page 53)
Coleslaw with Pineapple and Carrots (page 115)
Sliced Fruit with Yogurt and Honey

Tuesday Breakfast
Light Menu
Peachy Banana Shake (page 126)
Hearty Menu
Peachy Banana Shake (page 126)
Whole Wheat Toast with Butter or Margarine
Slice of Cooked Ham, heated

Tuesday Dinner
Light Menu
Fish Fillet Vinaigrette (page 62)
Sliced tomatoes with Dill
French Bread with Garlic Butter
Hearty Menu
Spicy Fish Stew (page 70)
Tossed Green Salad with Dressing and Dill
Pineapple Betty (page 145)

Wednesday Breakfast
Light Menu
Cranberry Juice
Whole Wheat Toast with Butter or Margarine
Slice of Cooked Ham
Hearty Menu
Cranberry Juice
Eggs with Corn and Bacon (page 89)
Whole Wheat Toast with Butter or Margarine

Wednesday Dinner
Light Menu
Tuna On a Muffin (page 73)
Carrot and Celery Sticks
1/2 Frozen Banana (page 126)
Hearty Menu
Pineapple Sweet and Sour Pork (page 34)
Brown Rice
Steamed Broccoli
1/2 Frozen Banana (page 126)

Thursday Breakfast
Light Menu
Pineapple Danish (page 133)
Hearty Menu
Orange Juice
Spicy Baked Pancake (page 139)

Thursday Dinner
Light Menu
Supper Salad (page 37)
French Bread, toasted
Cherry Crumb Crunch (page 160)

Hearty Menu
Tuna-Vegie Dish (page 70)
Carrot-Raisin Salad (page 116)
French Bread, toasted
Cherry Crumb Crunch (page 160)

Friday Breakfast
Light Menu
1/2 Grapefruit drizzled with Honey
Toasted English Muffin with Peanut Butter or Cream Cheese
Hearty Menu
1/2 Grapefruit drizzled with Honey
Eggs Benedict (page 87)

Friday Dinner
Light Menu
Shrimp-Corn Curry (page 75)
Best-Yet Walnut Bread (page 135)
Hearty Menu
Stuffed Green Peppers (page 28)
Spinach Salad with Oil and Vinegar Dressing
Best-Yet Walnut Bread (page 135)

Saturday Breakfast
Light Menu
Pineapple Smoothie (page 125)
Whole Wheat Toast with Butter or Margarine
Hearty Menu
Scrambled Eggs with Cheese and Dill
Blueberry Flummery (page 143)
Hazel's Quick Coffee Cake (page 134)

Saturday Dinner
Light Menu
Turkey Joes (page 55)
Cranberry Sauce
Steamed Green Peas with Chopped Mint
Edith's Oatmeal Cookies (page 161)
Hearty Menu
Stuffed Cornish Game Hen (page 51)
Brown Rice with dash of **Mixed Herbs (page 13)**
Steamed Green Peas with Chopped Mint
Aunt Esther's Wacky Cake (page 149)

Week 3

Sunday Breakfast
Light Menu
Baked Apple (page 124)
Hearty Menu
Fruit Juice
Hot Cereal with Raisins and Chopped Dates

Sunday Dinner
Light Menu
Succotash Ham (page 33)
Tossed Green Salad with French Dressing
Peanut Butter Squares (page 156)
Hearty Menu
Ham-Stuffed Squash (page 36)
Tossed Green Salad with Cucumber and Tomato Wedges
Apple-Cran Crisp (page 143)

Monday Breakfast
Light Menu
Orange Juice
Bagel with Cream Cheese and Jam

Hearty Menu
Orange Juice
Whole Wheat Toast with Butter or Margarine
Onion-Pepper Omelet (page 80)

Monday Dinner
Light Menu
Turkey Patties with Onion and Sage (page 55)
Tomato Wedges on fresh spinach, with fresh basil leaves if available
Hot French Bread
Fresh Orange Segments
Hearty Menu
Oriental Beef (page 23)
Rice
Steamed Broccoli
Fresh Orange Segments

Tuesday Breakfast
Light Menu
Tomato Juice with Dash of Hot Pepper Sauce
Super-Muffins (page 129)
Hearty Menu
Fruit Juice
Cold Cereal with Blueberries
Super-Muffin (page 129) with Peanut Butter

Tuesday Dinner
Light Menu
Tomato-Egg Bake (page 80)
Slice of Rye Bread with Butter or Margarine
Blueberry Sweet Bread (page 137)
Hearty Menu
Fish in Creamy Mushroom Sauce (page 67)
Grated Carrot Salad (page 123)
Blueberry Sweet Bread (page 137)

Wednesday Breakfast
Light Menu
Applesauce with Raisins
Whole Wheat Toast
Hearty Menu
Baked Apple (page 124)
Wheat Sticks (page 132)

Wednesday Dinner
Light Menu
French Onion Soup (page 98)
Mixed Fresh Greens — Lettuce, Spinach, Kale, Parsley
Date-Nut Squares (page 148)
Hearty Menu
Chicken Liver Special (page 50)
Waldorf Delight (page 117)
Hot French Bread
Steamed Carrots
Date-Nut Squares (page 148)

Thursday Breakfast
Light Menu
Yogurt with Chopped Fresh Fruit or Berries
English Muffin
Hearty Menu
Fruit or Berries
Broccoli and Egg (page 83)
Whole Wheat Toast

Thursday Dinner
Light Menu
Onions au Gratin (page 107)
Apple-Carrot Slaw (page 117)
Fruit Sorbet (page 146)

Hearty Menu
Turkey Tetrazzini (page 47)
Apple-Carrot Slaw (page 117)
Fruit Sorbet (page 146) and cookie

Friday Breakfast
Light Menu
Grapefruit Juice
Whole Wheat Toast with Cheese Slice
Hearty Menu
Grapefruit Juice
Cranberry Pears (page 125)
Toast with Grated or Sliced Cheese

Friday Dinner
Light Menu
Double Cheese (page 83)
Chopped Greens Salad with French Dressing
Rye Crackers
Fresh Pear, quartered
Hearty Menu
Black Beans 'n Rice (page 115)
Chopped Greens Salad with French Dressing
Fresh Pear, quartered
Oat Wheat Cookies (page 152)

Saturday Breakfast
Light Menu
Pineapple Juice
Pineapple Danish (page 133)
Hearty Menu
Fruit Compote (mixture of fresh and canned fruits)
Whole Wheat Toast with Butter or Margarine
Slice of Hot, Cooked Ham

Saturday Dinner
Light Menu
Mildred's Tomato-Cheese Soup (page 96)
Crackers
Carrot Sticks
1/2 Banana, sliced and sprinkled with Almonds
Hearty Menu
Spicy Red Snapper (page 65)
Wilted Spinach with Garlic and Nuts (page 113)
Carrot Sticks
Apple Spice Cake (page 150)

Week 4

Sunday Breakfast
Light Menu
Orange Wheel Slices with Flaked Coconut
Whole Wheat Toast with Peanut Butter and Honey
Hearty Menu
Orange Slices with Flaked Coconut
Grandpa Hal's Waffles (page 131)
Bacon or Ham

Sunday Dinner
Light Menu
Chicken á la King (page 43)
Granny's Baking Powder Biscuits (page 134)
Steamed Peas, Fresh or Frozen
Hearty Menu
Chicken Curry (page 41)
Rice
Tossed Green Salad with Dressing
Yogurt Banana Split (page 153)

Monday Breakfast
Light Menu
Cold Cereal with Milk and Sliced Bananas
Hearty Menu
Hot Cereal with Milk, Honey, Raisins and Chopped Fresh or Frozen Fruit

Monday Dinner
Light Menu
Supper Salad (page 37)
Hot French Bread
Cookie
Hearty Menu
"No-Peek" Stew (page 18)
Granny's Baking Powder Biscuits (page 134)
Tossed Greens Salad
Fresh or Canned Fruit and Cookie

Tuesday Breakfast
Light Menu
Pineapple Smoothie (page 125)
Hearty Menu
Fruit Juice
Whole Wheat Toast with Butter or Margarine
Scrambled Eggs with Ham Bits and Chives or Green Onions

Tuesday Dinner
Light Menu
Spicy Fish Stew (page 70)
Whole Wheat Toast
Rich & Easy Chocolate Pudding (page 148)
Hearty Menu
Vegetable-Rice (page 112)
Fruit Salad: Orange, Banana, and Apple Sections on Lettuce
Rich & Easy Chocolate Pudding (page 148)

Wednesday Breakfast
Light Menu
Yogurt with Chopped Banana and Frozen Blueberries
Hearty Menu
Fruit Juice
Hot Cereal with Raisins
Toast or Muffin

Wednesday Dinner
Light Menu
Mushroom-Zucchini Frittata (page 91)
Cornmeal Biscuits (page 133)
Cookie
Hearty Menu
Meat Loaf (page 22)
Coleslaw with Pineapple and Carrots (page 115)
Betty's Lemon Cake Pudding (page 145)

Thursday Breakfast
Light Menu
Orange Juice
Super-Muffins (page 129)
Hearty Menu
Orange Juice
Bacon and Potato Eggs (page 84)
Whole Wheat Toast with Butter or Margarine and Jam

Thursday Dinner
Light Menu
Lentil Soup (page 100)
Crackers
Tossed Green Salad with Dressing
Fresh or Canned Pears
Hearty Menu
Chicken Marmalada (page 45)
Chilled Bean Salad (page 120)
Pink Poached Pears (page 146)

Friday Breakfast
Light Menu
Peachy Banana Shake (page 126)
Hearty Menu
Peaches with Flaked Coconut
Cheese Pudding (page 89)

Friday Dinner
Light Menu
Tasty Tuna (page 68)
Minty Fruit Salad (page 124)
Hearty Menu
Ginger Snapper (page 65)
Minty Fruit Salad (page 124)
White or Brown Rice
Steamed Green Beans
Star Cookies (page 160)

Saturday Breakfast
Light Menu
Fruit with Yogurt-Ginger Sauce (page 154)
Hearty Menu
Fruit with Yogurt-Ginger Sauce (page 154)
Poached Egg on Toast

Saturday Dinner
Light Menu
Fried Rice (page 118)
Carrot-Raisin Salad (page 116)
Hearty Menu
Chicken Milano (page 45)
Carrot-Raisin Salad (page 116)
Vera's Fresh Strawberry Pie (page 158)

Week 5

Sunday Breakfast
Light Menu
Grape Juice
Edith's Oatmeal Cookies (page 161) with Peanut Butter
Hearty Menu
Applesauce
Spicy Baked Pancakes
2 strips bacon

Sunday Dinner
Light Menu
Beef 'n Beans (page 21)
Whole-wheat Bread with Butter or Margarine
Spinach Salad
Yogurt Banana Split (page 153)
Hearty Menu
Zucchini Linguine (page 108)
Spinach Salad
Yogurt Banana Split (page 153)
Star Cookies (page 160)

Monday Breakfast
Light Menu
Orange Juice
Blueberry Oatmeal Muffins (page 138)
Hearty Menu
Orange Juice
Scrambled Egg with Dill and Chopped Green Onion
Blueberry Oatmeal Muffins (page 138)

Monday Dinner
Light Menu
Sausage with Pepper with Pepper and Mushrooms (page 35)
Sliced Tomato
Apple-Cran Crisp (Page 143)
Hearty Menu
Succotash Ham (page 33)
Sliced Tomato on Lettuce with Sweet Basil
Apple-Cran Crisp (page 143)

Tuesday Breakfast
Light Menu
Prune Juice
Egg-in-a-Nest (page 90)
Hearty Menu
Stewed Prunes with Apple Chunks
Oatcakes (page 132) with Maple Syrup or jam

Tuesday Dinner
Light Menu
Stir-Fried Chicken (page 51)
White or Brown Rice
Tangerine, peeled and sectioned
Hearty Menu
Aunt Kathy's You-Ought-To-Start-A-Restaurant Soup (page 99)
Carrot and Celery Sticks
Corn Chips
Tangerine segments

Wednesday Breakfast
Light Menu
1/2 Grapefruit sprinkled with sugar or honey
Super-Muffins (page 129)
Hearty Menu
1/2 Grapefruit sprinkled with sugar or honey
Scrambled Eggs with Bacon
Whole Wheat Toast with Marmalade

Wednesday Dinner
Light Menu
Chicken Salad (page 42)
Hot Cornmeal Biscuit (page 133)
Applesauce and Ginger Snaps
Hearty Menu
Chicken Cobbler (page 53)
Tossed Green Salad with Dressing
Frozen Fruity Yogurt (page 152)

Thursday Breakfast
Light Menu
Fruit Juice
Whole Wheat Toast with Cinnamon, Brown Sugar, and Chopped Nuts
Hearty Menu
Pineapple Juice
Hot Cereal with Oat Bran, Cinnamon, Raisins, and Brown Sugar

Thursday Dinner
Light Menu
Fish on Spinach (page 66)
Rye Toast
Green Pepper and Carrot Salad with Oil and Vinegar Dressing
Hearty Menu
Swiss Steak Special (page 19)
Mashed or Roasted Potatoes
Green Pepper and Carrot Salad
Coconut Squares (page 156)

Friday Breakfast
Light Menu
Frozen Fruity Yogurt (page 152) sprinkled with Crushed Dry Cereal (corn or wheat flakes or granola)
Hearty Menu
Grapefruit Juice
Scrambled Eggs with Grated Cheese
Orange-Honey Loaf slice

Friday Dinner
Light Menu
Egg Foo Yung (page 86)
White or Brown Rice
Sliced Orange
Hearty Menu
Salmon Steaks Superb (page 71) or **Dr. Bob's Salmon Loaf (page 72)**
Sliced Cucumbers with Dill
Steamed Green Beans
Edith's Oatmeal Cookies (page 161)
Sliced Orange

Saturday Breakfast
Light Menu
Orange Juice
Poached Egg on Whole Wheat Toast
Hearty Menu
Orange Juice
Soft-Boiled Egg
Whole Wheat Toast with Butter or Margarine and Jam
Sausage Patties

Saturday Dinner
Light Menu
Mashed Potatoes Plus (page 110)
Steamed Broccoli
Mixed Fruit Compote
Hearty Menu
Lentils and Rice (page 118)
Steamed Broccoli topped with Grated Cheese
Mixed Fruit Compote and Cookies

Week 6

Sunday Breakfast
Light Menu
Pineapple Smoothie
Whole Wheat Toast
Hearty Menu
Pineapple Juice
Baked Potato Topped with Bacon Bits and Grated Cheese

Sunday Dinner
Light Menu
Salmon with Cheese (page 69)
Steamed Peas
Chopped Spinach Salad
Hearty Menu
Baked Fish with Mushrooms and Tomato (page 68)
Boiled Potatoes
Chopped Spinach Salad
Apple Spice Cake (page 150)

Monday Breakfast
Light Menu
Cold Cereal with Milk and Chopped Berries, Peaches or Banana
Hearty Menu
Yogurt Banana Split (page 153)
Toasted English Muffin with Butter or Margarine

Monday Dinner
Light Menu
Corn Pudding (page 85)
Steamed Peas, garnished with Chopped Mint Leaves
Peanut Butter Squares (page 156)

Hearty Menu
Spanish Rice (page 114)
Tossed Green Salad with Cucumber Slices
Peanut Butter Squares (page 156)

Tuesday Breakfast
Light Menu
Applesauce Topped with Chopped Nuts and Raisins
Whole Wheat Toast
Hearty Menu
Grapefruit Juice
Favorite Pancakes with Jam, Fruit Purée or Applesauce
Lean Cooked Ham Slice

Tuesday Dinner
Light Menu
Swiss Eggs (page 81)
Tomato, Cucumber and Radish Salad
Hearty Menu
Hamburger Stew (page 29)
Tomato, Cucumber and Radish Salad
Granny's Baking Powder Biscuits (page 134)
Ice cream or Frozen Yogurt

Wednesday Breakfast
Light Menu
Prune Juice
Yogurt with Chopped Dates, Raisins, and Crushed Cereal (flakes or granola)
Hearty Menu
Stewed Prunes with Lemon Wedge
Cheese Omelet
Whole Wheat Toast

Wednesday Dinner
Light Menu
Potato-Onion Soup (page 100)
Apple-Carrot Slaw (page 117)
Rye crackers
Hearty Menu
Chicken Cacciatore (page 43)
Noodles
Steamed Green Beans with Rosemary
Cherry Crumb Crunch (page 160)

Thursday Breakfast
Light Menu
Peachy Banana Shake (page 126)
Toast with Butter and Jam
Hearty Menu
Fresh or Canned Peaches
French Toast with Butter and Syrup or Brown Sugar or other favorite topping

Thursday Dinner
Light Menu
Spicy Red Snapper (page 65)
French Bread
Peach Half with Scoop of Cottage Cheese, on Lettuce
Best-Yet Walnut Bread (page 135)
Hearty Menu
Moon's Minestrone (page 97)
Garlic Bread
Tossed Greens Salad
Best-Yet Walnut Bread (page 135)

Friday Breakfast
Light Menu
Orange Juice
Bed-and-Breakfast Bran Muffins (page 130)

Hearty Menu
Orange Juice
Bed-and-Breakfast Bran Muffins
Chopped Ham, Stir-Fried and mixed with Pineapple Chunks

Friday Dinner
Light Menu
Chicken-Stuffed Tomato (page 52)
Hot French Bread
Prune-Apple Bars (page 157)
Hearty Menu
Chicken Parmesan (page 49)
Baked Potato
Steamed Celery Chunks with Sweet Basil
Prune-Apple Bars

Saturday Breakfast
Light Menu
Fruit Juice
Cold Cereal with Milk and Blueberries
Hearty Menu
Fruit Juice
Oatcakes (page 132) with Butter or Margarine and Syrup

Saturday Dinner
Light Menu
Chili Cheese (page 85)
Sliced Green Pepper and Red Onion with Oil and Vinegar Dressing
Frozen Banana Chunks (page 126)
Hearty Menu
Carolyn's Ratatouille (page 109)
Hot French Bread with Garlic Butter or Olive Oil
Rich & Easy Chocolate Pudding (page 148)

Cutting Back On Sodium

Health experts say that most of us take in more sodium than we need: from 2,300 to 6,900 milligrams per day. An adequate sodium intake per day for an adult is far less: 1,100 to 3,300 milligrams, according to the National Research Council. The American Heart Association recommends no more than 2,400 milligrams per day — that's about 1 teaspoon of salt.

Table salt, sodium chloride, is second only to sugar as a food additive. Sodium is also found in other common ingredients and additives such as baking soda, baking powder, sodium nitrite, and monosodium glutamate (MSG).

Too much sodium may contribute to high blood pressure, and many physicians recommend that we eat less of it. The easiest way is to cut down on salt. A few hints on decreasing sodium:

- Avoid "convenience foods," unless labeled low-sodium. Most frozen and canned dishes, such as pizzas, TV dinners, pies, and soups, have high amounts of sodium.

- Read labels on packaged foods and learn to recognize ingredients that contain sodium: salt, soy sauce, soda, MSG.

- Reduce or cut out the amount of salt in cooking.

- At the table, taste food before you add salt, or take the shaker off the table and use other flavor-enhancers instead, such as lemon juice, vinegar, and herbs.

Many of the recipes in this book are low to moderate in sodium content. Those that are especially low in sodium are listed on the following page. Others may be adjusted to lower-sodium diets simply by omitting salt and avoiding canned ingredients, which almost always contain sodium.

Herbs are creative, flavorful alternatives to salt. They can turn simple foods into gourmet delights that tempt the appetite and please the palate. Replace the salt in your diet with other seasonings and help keep your blood pressure down while you enhance your dining pleasure.

This chart will help you choose which herbs and spices to use

Beef	Bay leaf, chives, cloves, cumin, garlic, marjoram, savory, thyme, pepper, nutmeg.
Poultry	Lemon, garlic, sage, thyme, paprika, marjoram, rosemary, oregano, savory.
Fish	Lemon, curry, dry mustard, marjoram, chervil, dill, fennel, tarragon, garlic, parsley, thyme.
Lamb	Rosemary, garlic, ginger, pepper, savory, thyme, coriander, sage, mint, curry.
Pork/Ham	Cumin, garlic, ginger, mustard, pepper, savory, thyme, coriander, sage.
Cheese	Sweet basil, chervil, chives, curry, garlic, marjoram, dill, parsley, oregano, thyme.
Eggs	Sweet basil, dill, parsley, savory.

Bread	Caraway, poppy seed, marjoram, thyme.
Asparagus	Lemon, garlic.
Beans	Dill, lemon, marjoram, nutmeg.
Carrots	Marjoram, ginger.
Cucumbers	Chives, dill, garlic, vinegar.
Peas	Mint, parsley.
Potatoes	Chives, paprika, parsley, mace.
Squash	Cinnamon, ginger, mace, nutmeg.
Tomatoes	Sweet basil, marjoram, oregano, dill.
Fruits`	Cinnamon, cloves, ginger, mint.

Recipes in this book which are low or moderate in sodium are:

Low-Cholesterol Recipes

The latest evidence in nutritional studies shows that we have a better chance of preventing cardiovascular disease if we eat foods that are low in cholesterol or help reduce it. Cholesterol is a fatty substance the body needs, but when it's out of balance it can clog arteries, preventing the blood from flowing freely.

Many of the dishes in this book are low in cholesterol; the lowest are listed below. You can lower cholesterol intake even further by substituting low-cholesterol ingredients for high ones. The following charts show the foods to choose or avoid.

Check with your doctor if you are concerned about the cholesterol level in your diet.

Foods High In Cholesterol

Butter, lard, hard margarine
Peanut and palm oils (read labels for ingredients; many
      prepared foods contain these oils)
Salt pork, bacon, red meats
Gravies and sauces made with cream and/or cheese
All milk except skim
Whole-milk cheese
Egg yolk
Frankfurters, sausage, lunch meats
Poultry skin
Organ meats: heart, liver, brains, kidney
Corned beef, spareribs
Most frozen packaged dinners
Commercial biscuit and cake mixes, except angel food cake
Potato and corn chips, flavored crackers, pretzels
Sweet rolls, doughnuts, commercial cake and bread mixes

Cream soups
Avocado
Pies, cakes, cookies containing whole milk or egg yolk
Ice cream, ice milk, whipped cream, most non-dairy creamers
Chocolate, coconut, most candies
Cashew and macadamia nuts
Condiments: catsup, soy sauce, steak sauce, pickles, mustard

Foods Low In Cholesterol

Margarine high in polyunsaturated fats, such as:
    Fleishmann's
    Mazola
    Nucoa
    Saffola
    Chiffon (soft tub)
Polyunsaturated oils: safflower, corn, soybean
Monounsaturated oils: olive, canola
Fish oil
Non-dairy coffee creamers that contain soybean oil
Oats and oat bran
Poultry
Fresh or frozen vegetables
Fresh or frozen fruits
Fish, especially salmon and mackerel
Wheat bran and corn bran
Garlic
Dried beans and peas
Egg whites
Dry curd cottage cheese, low-fat cheese
Skim milk, non-fat yogurt, skimmed buttermilk
Barley, rice, pasta
Gelatin, sherbet, pudding made with skim milk, angel food cake
Homemade soups
Vinegar, herbs, spices, honey, jam, syrup

Recipes in this book which are low in cholesterol include:

Recipes To Share With Grandchildren

These dishes are fun for grandparents to serve to grandchildren, or for them to make together:

Index

Recipes are listed in alphabetical order by section.

Desserts

Eggs & Cheese

Pork & Ham

Poultry

Seafood

Soups

Vegetables & Fruits

Notes

Notes

Did you like *The Healthy Seniors Cookbook?*

Do you need more copies for friends and relatives? Of course you do! Order directly from the publisher at www.geroproducts.com, through your local bookstore, or use the order form below (may be photocopied).

Also, you may be interested in our other books and gifts:

Qty ___

The Healthy Seniors Cookbook: Ideal Meals and Menus for People Over Sixty (Or Any Age) by Marilyn McFarlane - $19.95
Whether cooking for yourself, your spouse, or visiting grandchildren, this book features an easy-to-read, easy-to-use format that provides flavorful meals and simple, fast cooking methods.

Qty ___

Romance is in the Air: A Senior Love Story by Ginger Binkley- $25.95
Can Ginny Baylor find the love of a lifetime when she enters the dating scene at age sixty-five? Can retired pilot Bill Sutton provide her with the love she needs when romance is in the air?

Qty ___

Seniors in Love: A Second Chance for Single, Divorced and Widowed Seniors by Robert Wolley - $19.95
This well-reviewed book deals with the emotional, financial, physical, and other relevant issues facing seniors when considering a new, intimate relationship.

Qty —

The Greatest Companion: Reflections on Life, Love and Marriage After 60 by Robert Wolley - $19.95

Through prose and poetry, this book explores the joys of late-in-life love, provides reminders of what such a love needs to flourish, and reflects upon love's agelessness.

Qty —

ABC's for Seniors: Successful Aging Wisdom from an Outrageous Gerontologist by Ruth Jacobs - $19.95

In this book, Dr. Jacobs presents the essentials that enable a reader to harvest life fully for creative, healthy, successful, vigorous, and meaningful aging.

Qty —

Seniors in Love car magnet - $11.95

Show the world that love knows no age! An ideal wedding or anniversary gift! Measures six by four inches, in red, white, and gold. Removable. Fits any RV!

Qty —

"Golf is a good walk spoiled" mug - $9.95

Mark Twain said it, but it's as true today as it was 100 years ago! Illustration and quote, printed in black on both sides.

Qty —

"Grow old along with me" mug - $9.95
Robert Browning said it, but it's as true today
as it was 100 years ago! Illustration and
quote, printed in black on both sides. Truly,
"the best is yet to be"

Qty —

Rock, Paper, Seniors game - $19.95
A reminiscence-based card game for seniors
which includes "rock" (who you are at the
core), "paper" (documentable events in your life),
and "senior" (existential) questions. Ideal for work
with senior groups or family gatherings.

Name   _____

Address   _____

City/State/Zip   _____

Please mark the products you want, and their quantity (Missouri
residents only please add 5.25% sales tax).

There is no charge for shipping and handling, and all orders are
shipped from Greentop, Missouri (population 427).

Send check or money order to:
Hatala Geroproducts
PO Box 42
Greentop, MO 63546

What makes Hatala Geroproducts different?

Hatala Geroproducts of Greentop, Missouri, was founded in 2002. An independent company, Hatala Geroproducts publishes books, games, magnetic signs, and greeting cards primarily for seniors. The focus is on relationships: with spouses, lovers, other seniors, grandchildren, and adult children.

• All products are "age positive", which means that they are respectful to seniors, and focus on the positive aspects of aging.

• All books are "larger print" for easier reading.

• Books are written by senior authors for senior readers.

• All products are developed with the help of academic gerontologists and seniors themselves.

• Hatala Geroproducts is dedicated to remain an earth-friendly, sustainable, carbon-neutral company.

We thank you for your continued support!

If you have any questions or comments, feel free to contact me personally at mark@geroproducts.com

Mark Hatala, Ph.D.
President, Hatala Geroproducts
Professor of Psychology, Truman State University

Printed in the United States
109887LV00004B/370-387/A